'RUTH-LESS'
AND FAR FROM HOME

With best wishes,

Kevin Watson

September 2000.

Kevin Watson

'RUTH-LESS' AND FAR FROM HOME
was first published in the year 2000

Published by Kevin Watson, Eastbourne
First Edition

Printed in England by
The Finmere Press Ltd

Reprographics by
Rare Repro, Hailsham, East Sussex

Cover Design by Gary Lloyd and Kevin Loats

ISBN   0-9538390-0-1

This book is dedicated to Arthur King

CONTENTS

ACKNOWLEDGEMENTS

I would like to sincerely thank 'Will' Lundy, the historian of the 44th Bombardment Group, for his invaluable assistance and support during my researches into the history of 'Ruth-Less' and her crews. Also Steve Adams the UK representative for the 44th BG who has also worked tirelessly to provide me with extra information, plus most of the superb photographs included in this publication which he has kindly loaned me on behalf of the 44th BG Veterans Association and from his own collection.

My thanks to George Dixon and Councillor Ron Parsons for their vision in seeing through the 'Ruth-Less' memorial project with me.

Jefferson Collard, Eastbourne Borough Council's Historic Buildings advisor for his keen professional interest in the project.

Also, special thanks to the following for their willing and enthusiastic help with the preparation of this book, to whom I am eternally grateful:

Merrill Berthrong, Martin Bowman, Ollie Bowling, Richard 'Dick' Butler, Art Grimes, James Caillier, Maurice Hall, James McAtee, William 'Bill' Strong, Ruth Swanson and Michael Longenecker.

FOREWORD

My mother, now 92 years of age, was walking home from a shopping expedition with my youngest brother in a push-chair, when the American bomber 'Ruth-Less' flew over the town, in it's attempt to make an emergency landing at the Friston air-strip. My mother and brother waved to the members of the crew as they stood at the waist-windows of the aircraft. It crashed soon after.

My other brother, still only a boy, later joined others in their search of the hillside where the Liberator crashed for parts of the 'plane, and returned home with small pieces of mica, from which my father fashioned a small cross that my mother cherishes to this day.

It was not difficult therefore, for me some fifty years later and as Mayor of Eastbourne, to respond to the request which I received from Kevin Watson, in giving my support to the project establishing the memorial near Butts Brow in memory of the ten young American airmen, which was dedicated during the fiftieth anniversary of 'Victory in Europe'.

These ten American crewmen became special to the citizens of Eastbourne, not just because they died in our town, but because, in their last moments, they and the residents of my town waved to and cheered each other.

Those young Americans will always remain special to Eastbourne.

RON PARSONS – APRIL 1997
Mayor of Eastbourne 1994 - 96

The 'Ruth-Less' Fellowship

We sit and view the Sussex Downs,
At grazing sheep, as seagulls cry,
Yet some of us hear other sounds,
For brave young men, destined to fly.

They came to fight besides the Few,
To ease the burden of our pain,
They were our cousins, staunch and true,
And each day we see them again.

We knew the trouble which they shared,
The engines coughed amid the cloud,
We hoped their lives would all be spared,
And ardent prayers were said aloud.

But 'Ruth-less' could not make the height,
And through the mist she came to rest,
Upon a hill, within our sight,
And God's hand rose on those he blessed.

They died upon a foreign field,
Defending freedom to the last,
For what the daylight then revealed,
Were friends together, hands held fast.

Their youthful spirits walk there still,
Past flowers blooming in the sun,
They smile down from Willingdon Hill,
Aware of duty proudly done.

DOUG THOMAS, 1995

INTRODUCTION

In this book, I have endeavoured to illustrate the adventures of one aircraft amongst thousands. The hopes, prayers and lives of the crews rested on the wings of 'Ruth-Less', the skill of her pilots and to a greater degree, 'Lady luck'.

To contemplate that this kind of tragedy occurred in so many other individual cases, sums up the sheer waste of war as young lives were cut tragically short and families suffered subsequent trauma and sorrow.

I do not claim to be an expert on the 8th American Army Air Force. I have endeavoured to relate technical and historical matters as accurately as possible. Any unforeseen errors are entirely of my own making and for which I apologise.

Kevin Watson – March 2000

Chapter One
DISCOVERY OF THE WRECKAGE

M Y parents had a large house constructed in 1968 on an elevated plot of land in the neck of a spur on The South Downs named The Combe, on the Ratton Manor Estate, Eastbourne. The house backed directly onto the woods which clothed the steep 500-foot east-facing slope of the hills at Willingdon.

The Combe, meaning 'a valley in the side of a hill', was a tract of land sold off in plots, for the private development of luxury houses from the estate which once belonged to Lord Willingdon and his family. Lord Willingdon was one of the last Viceroys to India and a former Governor General of Canada. During the Second World War, his attractive and substantial manor house with it's elegant gardens and terraces, was commandeered for use by officers of the Canadian Army. The Combe itself was a natural range for the practice firing of mortars and small arms fire, being secluded and sheltered.

Unfortunately, the boisterous Canadians did not have a great deal of respect for their beautiful surroundings and during a particularly exuberant party, the building caught fire and burned out of control. After the war, the remains of the house were bulldozed and cleared down to the foundations.

When I arrived on the scene in my early adolescence, great fun was had by myself and two friends who also lived in The Combe, as we played and explored the ruins of the manor house with it's overgrown gardens now thick with weeds and saplings. There was a

1

beautiful outdoor swimming pool inlaid with a mosaic of blue ceramic tiles, but sadly filled in, as it occupied a large part of the back garden of a new house in Upper Ratton Drive. In what were the grounds fronting the house there was an ornamental pond, which I imagined at one time filled with exotic fish, but now just containing mud and debris. What a pity there was not sufficient money to repair the estate after the war.

During the long summer holidays, my friends and I would build camps in the woods, some either up stout beech trees or excavated underground. In the course of our digging around the sides of The Combe, we found what we thought was a small bomb, it was quite rusty but intact. A telephone call to the Bomb Disposal Squad brought a swift response and the offending device was removed and destroyed.

When we learned that the Canadians had used The Combe as a firing range, we intensified our searches and came across many more mortar bombs and even some boxes of live ammunition simply buried in the ground. Due to soil erosion, we became so proficient at finding this ammunition, that one weekend the Bomb Disposal Squad attended to our discoveries three times. Such was our success, Southern Television as it was known then, did a special feature on our exploits.

The Combe nestles close to a high point of The Downs known as Butts Brow, which is easily identified from many miles around by the patch of trees that sit on the top. The steep and high hillside on the southern side of Butts Brow, which overlooks the Willingdon Golf Course was, as we would soon learn, the site of a major tragedy when an American aircraft crashed there in February 1944.

As our explorations took us around this side of the hill, we were thrilled to discover an underground WWII bunker, right by the Bridal Path that leads up from Ratton to the top of the Downs. Now concentrating our operations in this area, we soon came to a range of saplings at the base of the hill, which on further investigation disclosed pieces of twisted and rusting metal. Some of the large pieces of this scrap were of a light grey colour caused by exposure to the elements, which we knew must be aluminium. Further expeditions, when we were better equipped with spades and trowels, produced a window frame, pieces of flight instruments and a whole belt of live ammunition!

As this area was too inaccessible for anyone to simply dump rubbish there, we quickly deduced that we had discovered the wreckage of an airplane, but what type? The inquiries that we made only partially satisfied our curiosity. Eventually we were told that the parts of an aircraft lying around were from an American Liberator bomber, which we knew to be a large four engined aircraft.

And that is how the situation was left. After a few more weeks of digging, it all became rather hard work for the fruits the terrain reluctantly released from its grasp. It also dawned on us after our initial excitement, that we could be desecrating an area where some people had actually died. Superstition then got the better of young under-developed minds and we aborted our excavations.

That was back in 1971, the memories of which lay locked away in my subconscious, when the key to unlocking them came about in the form of an article in my local newspaper. In February 1994 on the back page of The Eastbourne Herald, there was a photograph of an elderly gentleman named Arthur King posing on the Downs with a United States flag. The story was about how for the last fifty years, in all weathers, Mr King had laid flowers on Remembrance Sunday at the crash site, in memory of the ten young American airmen who perished there. A chill swept up my spine, here is someone who may be able to answer those questions which my friends and I had raised all those years ago. After finding Arthur's telephone number with some relief in the local directory, I gave him a call. After a brief explanation for this 'phone call out of the blue, he was delighted that I had contacted him and stated that he had received several other calls in relation to the bomber story.

Arthur mentioned that on the 2nd February 1944, he was in the back garden of the house he still resides in to this day, when he saw the Liberator fly over very low. He did not have much detail on the circumstances that caused the aircraft to crash, other than the weather that day was very poor, with low cloud sitting on top of the Downs, driving rain and high winds. We agreed to meet sometime soon, to go up to the crash site and correlate the exact position of the impact, but in the meantime I would attempt some research in order to discover more about this aircraft.

So if you need to find out information regarding a WWII aircraft and it's crew, where do you start? Are those records locked away in

3

vaults for many more years under an act of state security or fifty-year rule? What about surviving relatives of the crew? There must be sisters, brothers, widows and children still alive somewhere. Did they know how or where their loved ones died? The task ahead seemed awesome, but undaunted I took the first steps by writing to the Imperial War Museum, to see if they could offer any assistance. Eventually I received a reply from the Records Department giving me an address for The Maxwell Airforce Base in Alabama, USA and the suggestion that I should place an advertisement in the Airforce Magazine, as an attempt to contact relatives of the crew. I quickly fired off two letters and waited hopeful of any replies. By this time the month of June had arrived and taking advantage of a fine summer's day, I rang Arthur King and arranged to collect him for the drive via Butts Lane to the Butts Brow car park and the short walk along to the crash site.

When I rang Arthur's doorbell a cheerful voice called out and on opening the door a sprightly octogenarian was revealed. He had a warm and friendly disposition, his face was weathered by many years out in the elements as a window cleaner, and his bright and sparkling eyes had clearly marked laughter lines around them. Arthur related how he had lived in Victoria Drive since the day his terraced house was constructed in the 1930's. He laughed as he said how his window cleaning career had been responsible for wearing the joints out in his arms, but he made light of his discomfort and the conversation soon changed to the main reason for our meeting.

Arthur recalled how for all these years he had been motivated to keep the memory of the American crew alive, by placing flowers up there on the Downs. He was saddened at how those young men had died, fighting to protect our country and civilisation so many miles from their own homes and families. In the trauma of war, he thought that probably their relatives did not know exactly what had happened and on their behalf, after the end of hostilities, he would honour their bravery and memory, by visiting the crash site each year on Remembrance Sunday.

"Perhaps one day" he said, "their families may get to learn how much I and the British people do care for the sacrifice of their sons, husbands and brothers, up there on that desolate spot". How prophetic his words would turn out to be.

Surveying the Downs, Arthur and I quickly agreed on the actual crash position give or take a few yards, and from that vista point overlooking the Ocklynge and Old Town areas of Eastbourne, you could visually depict the likely route the aircraft flew before impact. But where was it going and why? As I looked down the hillside, I could see the area of saplings at the base of the hill, where nearly a quarter of a century ago, my friends and I had found the wreckage. You could imagine by following a straight line down the hill, how the crash debris had accumulated at the bottom due to the combined natural forces of gravity and soil erosion.

Arthur King at the crash site pointing in the direction
'Ruth-Less' flew from the coast.

I took some photographs of the area, then took Arthur home. I felt quite elated and excited about our afternoon on the Downs, but tamed with a slight disappointment that my researches had apparently come to a dead end already. Perhaps I should try another tack, or wait a little longer until I get a response from my advertisement in the Airforce Magazine? I'll plan a new strategy just in case, but as it happened it wasn't needed.

My occupation flying for British Airways, has taken me all over the world from Anchorage in Alaska down to the Falkland Islands. Being away from home for at least half of the year can upset your social calendar, and 'Sod's Law' usually means that I miss some important family event from time to time. For someone to turn-up at my house, to find me either in the country or not off out somewhere, is pretty rare, hence I was delighted to be visited by George Dixon, a retired schoolmaster who had taught me some years ago at the Eastbourne Grammar School.

George (he insisted I dropped the Mr. Dixon) presented me with a magazine cutting which had been pasted on to a postcard. The

Arthur King at the crash site

6

coincidence which had caused our paths to cross, was that George had spent a number of his early years as a teacher in Norfolk. This was not long after the Second World War, during which time Eastern England became a land-borne carrier for the mighty American Eighth Army Airforce. George had retained an interest and knowledge of our allies through his contacts with an American veterans association. 'Pete' Henry, a former B-24 pilot of 506 squadron, 44th Bombardment Group, had seen my advert in the Airforce magazine and forwarded it to George. At last my initial researches had prompted a response.

During our conversation, George related how he had read about a Liberator bomber in a book entitled 'Eighth Airforce Bomber Stories'. The aircraft had crashed in Eastbourne on the 2nd February 1944, and eyewitnesses to the accident had contacted the author after he had placed an advertisement in the local newspaper. One of those who responded was Arthur King. When George discovered how Arthur had been placing flowers at the crash site for all those years, he arranged the photo opportunity with the Eastbourne Herald newspaper, bringing to the attention of the reporter Arthur's dedication to the deceased crewmembers and suggesting that the feature was published as near as possible to the 50th anniversary of the accident.

It was fascinating chatting with George about the aircraft and to compare our information, which incidentally was complimentary in that we both had something the other did not know of. I suggested that if we could motivate enough public interest, perhaps a perma- nent memorial could be established on the crash site. George was somewhat sceptical of the feasibility of such a project and the logis- tics to fulfil this scheme seemed formidable. We agreed to work together, keeping each other posted as information was received.

Soon after my meeting with George, a package arrived from the USA containing a copy of a Missing Air-Crew Report Form, which included the names of the crew who died at Butts Brow and some brief information of the time and location of the crash. The former B- 24 pilot 'Pete' Henry, replying to a letter of mine, put me in touch with the historian of the 44th Bombardment Group. I had struck gold again.

'Will' Lundy was an Assistant Crew Chief, maintaining B-24's for the duration of the war. He now lives in San Bernardino, California

7

along with his British born wife Irene, who he met during his tour of duty. 'Will' had a vast amount of information at his disposal and it was not long before many copies of official documents were being airmailed to me.

Probably the most important discovery that 'Will' made, was the tracking down of the co-pilots sister.'Will' had written to the head postmaster of the town given as the co-pilots hometown. Fortunately the postmaster remembered that the family no longer lived in De Smet and forwarded 'Will's letter to Ruth W. Swanson in Lake Preston, South Dakota.

On receiving this information I couldn't wait to get away on my next trip to New York, so that I could attempt to trace Ruth's telephone number through directory enquiries. I arrived at John F.

Ruth Swanson.

8

Kennedy Airport on the 8th November 1994 and it was late afternoon local time before I reached my hotel in Downtown Manhattan. Luckily Ruth's telephone number was not ex-directory and I immediately dialled the code.

After a copy of rings Ruth answered speaking in a rather quavery voice. I felt quite nervous and was not sure what her reaction would be to my surprise 'phone call. Talking with Ruth was slow progress initially, as she had a speech impediment caused when her vocal chords were cauterised forty odd years ago. Ruth was delighted that I had contacted her and to learn that I had been conducting some research into her brother's death. She was able to give me some valuable information concerning the circumstances of the crash, which was originally sent to her parents. She and her brother Orville Wulff were very close she explained, and they had a strong brother-sister bond between them. A few weeks later in a letter, Ruth related to me how she had written to her brother on the 3rd February 1944, describing a jaunt in the frozen countryside of her native South Dakota, and commenting on the scenic beauty of the ice-glazed trees. This letter was later returned marked "deceased".

The day before she wrote that letter, Ruth told me how she had lost a brooch fashioned like a pair of silver wings, in the deep snow as she left her house. Because it was a gift from Orville, it took quite a search to recover it. This event was later construed by her Church Minister as an omen.

The news of Orville's death did not reach the family until the 16th February. Ruth and her husband were looking up at the night sky around 9pm that night, when they saw a gold cross through the full moon for several minutes from their yard. Ruth has a clipping from a newspaper indicating that a similar phenomenon occurred over England at that time.

Having made contact with Ruth, I was spurred on to find out what truly happened to Orville's aircraft and the circumstances of the crash. Information was coming in almost daily as I contacted veterans of the 44th Bombardment Group and 'Will' Lundy forwarded copies of de-classified documents from the National Archives in Washington D.C.

After nearly five years of research, the story of the B-24D Liberator bomber 'Ruth-Less' and that fateful day, February 2nd 1944, can now be told . . .

Chapter 2

PREPARING FOR COMBAT

'**R**UTH-LESS' was an early specification B-24D Liberator, full serial number B-24D-25-CO4124282. Later derivatives became B-24H's and so on, as improvements were implemented to the original design specification. The Consolidated Aircraft Company constructed 'Ruth-Less' during November 1942, at their factory in San Diego, California. Consolidated had made successful flying boats in the past and looking at the B-24, the flying boat ancestry is apparent in it's design. The Liberator was not such a photogenic aircraft as the Boeing B-17 Flying Fortress of 'Memphis Belle' fame. On the ground, the Liberators were often compared to beached whales, but in the air they had poise, precision and punch.

Curiously, the Liberator was designed to a French Government specification issued in May 1938 for a heavy bomber. Later in March 1939, the US Army Corps also put forward a requirement for a bomber with a better performance than the B-17, which was already flying. Consolidated incorporated all their winning features in long range aircraft design, into a landplane version of their Model 29 flying boat otherwise known as the PB2Y. In September 1939, the French signed a production contract for 139 aircraft, but after the fall of France in June 1940, Britain took over the order for those LB-30 or Mark 1 'Liberators' as christened by the RAF.

Being a later design, the Liberator had the 'Davis' designed wing, which had a very high wing loading for its time, necessitating long paved runways for take-off and landing. David R. Davis was near destitute when he sold his innovative new wing design to Consolidated in 1937. Reuben H.Fleet the President of Consolidated, was sceptical of the inventors claims, but wind tunnel tests later proved that the slender wing with its sharp camber and constant taper from root to tip provided superior lift.

The B-24's outperformed the B-17's in nearly every way as they flew higher, faster and further. The long elliptical 'Davis' wing also suited extended over-water patrols at low or medium altitudes. Liberators were utilised effectively in the Pacific, where the Japanese feared their masthead bombing technique.

The Liberator could carry 15 X 250 lb bombs, or several one ton blockbusters up to a maximum range of 3,000 miles, at a cruising speed of around 220-mph. Although an effective design at lower altitudes, the 'Davis' wing made the Liberator a less forgiving aircraft to fly than the B-17 and difficult to control in formation, requiring a higher degree of airmanship. The control surfaces did not have servos or power assist, so the B-24 was very heavy to fly manually. Thankfully the aircraft had an efficient autopilot. Liberator pilots would comment that manoeuvring the '24 in the air, was like sitting on your front porch and flying the rest of the house from there. On take-off as the wheels lifted from the runway, some pilots would prudently touch the brakes to stop the wheels rotating as the undercarriage was retracted. This was due to each of the main undercarriage struts retracting unevenly and the associated gyroscopic effect of the wheels spinning, could de-stabilise the heavily laden bomber at that critical time.

Early 'D' versions of the Liberator or B-24, had the uprated turbo-supercharged Pratt and Whitney 1,200 horsepower R-1830-43 Twin Wasp engines, distinguished by having side mounted oil coolers which necessitated the elliptical cowling around the radial engines. The B-24D had a gross all up weight of 56,000lbs. By 1941 2,738 Liberators had been constructed, with 2,425 of them made by Consolidated-Vultee at San Diego. If there were the letters 'CO' in the serial number of a B-24, this would indicate that the aircraft was built by Consolidated, although other production lines were being opened by Convair in Fort Worth, Texas; the Douglas Company in Tulsa and at the end of 1942, the Ford Motor Company had a new plant constructed at Willow Run, Michigan, at a cost then of U$165 million. In early 1943, a fifth production line was established by

North American at Dallas. Altogether 18,188 B-24 Liberators were built before production finally ended on the 31st May 1945, far more than any other aircraft produced during WW II.

The Liberator was not able to sustain and withstand the punishment of enemy fire that a B-17 could, and was less survivable in a crash landing or ditching. The B-24's fuselage and tail surfaces were exceedingly strong. Cases were on record of Liberators coming safely home with fully 50% of the tail shot away and the fuselage completely Swiss-cheesed. More vulnerable were the wings, especially under the tremendous overloadings common during the latter years of the European war. Almost twice the length of the fuselage, the slim wing carried such a high wingloading, that often a minor hit was sufficient to throw the aircraft totally and irrecoverably out of control.

The propellers fitted to early production Liberators, were nicknamed 'toothpick' propellers because of their sleeker blade design, but soon these were replaced with a wider chord 'paddle' type, which provided a significant boost in performance. The most obvious design difference between the B-17 Flying Fortress and the Liberator, was that the B-24 had twin fins. Later derivatives would eventually go to a single large fin assembly which provided greater stability. Also the Liberator had a tricycle undercarriage system while most other aircraft of that time, especially the larger ones like the British Avro Lancaster, were tail draggers. This landing gear arrangement enabled the B-24 to have a better crosswind capability in take-offs and landings. The nosewheel was vulnerable to poor surfaces and could be easily sheared off by a pothole or by getting bogged down in a marshy grass landing strip, which was a further reason why Liberators operated from paved runways.

During the 1930's, the American bombing strategy was to drop ordinance with great precision from an altitude sufficiently high, to make enemy groundfire ineffective, allowing the bombers a clear run at the target:-

"Which pickle would you like to hit?" was Carl Norden's response when asked if his new bomb sight could drop a bomb into a pickle barrel from 20,000 feet. Norden filed the patent for his invention on the 27th May 1932 and the sight was manufactured by the Victor Adding Machine Company. The Norden bombsight fitted to the B-24 and the B-17 was a mechanical analogue computer, designed to determine the exact point bombs needed to be released to hit the target. Norden's invention was a pivotal improvement over other bombsights. After being electronically connected to the aircraft's autopilot, it could measure the aircraft's groundspeed as the target was locked-in. It also provided true air speed, wind speed, wind direction, angle of drift, and taking all of these factors into account, automatically dropped the bombs, thus eliminating most human error. This piece of equipment enabled American bombers to carry out high altitude precision strategic bombing, and was considered one of their most highly guarded secrets by the US throughout WW II.

With their new top secret 'Norden' bombsight, the American Army Airforce's confidence in this piece of equipment was based on the theory that their bombing for the most part, would be pursued during daylight hours. To inhibit attack from enemy fighter aircraft, the American bombers boasted a quite comprehensive amount of firepower and when flying in formation, it was thought the enemy would not dare to penetrate their enfilade defensive firepower. Carrying those guns and the ammunition for them, severely compromised the bomb load of the American aircraft, of which the B-24, although superior to a B-17, could only uplift less than half the weight of bombs that the RAF's Avro Lancaster was capable of.

The Americans faith in their precision and daylight bombing tactics, were themselves blown away in the heat of actual combat. Accurate bombing with a sophisticated bombsight was fine as long as you can see the aiming point, if any cloud obscured the area you either had to find another target of opportunity or abort. The Germans soon developed radar controlled 88mm and 110mm anti-aircraft guns, which could accurately bracket or box the airspace around a bomber with flak, even at heights up to 25,00 feet or more. German fighter aircraft found the weakest area in which to attack the huge American bomber formations by flying suicidally straight at the aircraft firing their guns and cannons, before rolling inverted at the last moment and diving away. Later derivatives of the B-17 and B-24 had motorised turrets fitted to their noses firing four cannons, but in the case of the B-24H, the extra weight of this adaptation made the aircraft even worse to fly by effecting it's centre of gravity adversely and reducing it's top speed by a margin.

In spite of grievous losses, the Americans persisted with their daylight bombing offensive throughout the war, whilst the RAF appalled at their early rate of attrition, perfected night-time bombing. The attraction of blasting the Germans 'round the clock', ensured the continuation of their respective strategies.

When the USA eventually threw it's hat fully into the ring after the bombing of Pearl Harbour, the recruitment and training of aircrew in the 'States became a priority. Learning to fly aircraft like the Boeing Stearman biplane initially, the student pilots would quickly pass through their flying syllabus and then be selected by their instructors on whether they would become a fighter, bomber or transport aircraft pilot. Generally the pilots with the greater aptitude went on to fly fighters, which was the dream of most of the students being perceived to be the more glamorous option. Being a bomber pilot was a grim prospect, as the word soon got back from the European Theatre of Operations as to your chances of survival.

1st Lt. Frank Slough after completing his training with 308 squadron, was assigned to 506 sq. in the 44th Bombardment Group of the 8th United States Army Airforce, as the 506th were a couple of crews short. Slough's falling into disfavour with the 308th Group commander prompted this move. During the last month of 1942, 506 sq. were still at the Pueblo Army Airbase, Colorado with Frank Slough and his crew continuing their training duties. By the year's end, the combat crews had become welded into efficient fighting teams, destined to achieve an outstanding operational record.

It was during the month of December that an accident occurred, which resulted in Lt. Slough and his Flight Engineer James Caillier becoming the first squadron personnel to receive decorations for heroism. As he was flying his B-24 in formation on a practice bombing mission, after 'bombs away', one of the other B-24's broke formation and suddenly came up from under and in front of Slough's aircraft.

Flight Engineer James Caillier remembers the events aboard Slough's Liberator on the 23rd December 1942:

> We had just been flying in formation and dropping 'Baby Blues' (practice bombs), this we were told, was the way we would be bombing in combat. I stood between the pilot and co-pilot and heard Frank (Slough) call the other

two ships. We were the lead and he told them that we would break formation and fly single file to the practice gunnery on the side of the canyon where there was a target to aim at. I saw the two wingmen break off as if to trail us. I thought that I had time to go to the back of the ship as I often did, to check out the fellows and look around. One of the gunners was afraid of flying and sometimes talking seemed to calm him down.

All of a sudden, the aircraft shuddered as if it had struck a brick wall. It knocked us all down in the back of the ship. The alarm was ringing and I helped two of the crewmen to their feet. We started for the bomb bay in order to hang from the bomb rack to jump.

While in the bomb bay, I could see Slough in his seat and the Navigator lying in the crawl hole and shaking with fear. I went to assist the Navigator, but he was incoherent and couldn't jump. I helped him back into the flight deck. Frank saw us but made no comment. I headed for the nose where I found the Bombardier trapped with his legs outside the aircraft. He was in a wind tunnel, because where he was sitting, the ship was cracked like an egg.

I went back to the flight deck to tell Frank what I had found. His only response was "Didn't you hear the alarm?" I told him that I had. He then said to sit down and help him with the wheel. The aircraft was shaking very badly. Frank was cool, but was swearing about the 'chicken' co-pilot. We couldn't see forward because something was wrapped around us. I put my head out of the window and looked down to see where we were. It was then that I realised that we were pushing the tail end of another aircraft!

We started to fishtail so that we could see a little ahead. Each manoeuvre was very dangerous since we were on full power, but just about staying airborne. Nevertheless, we had to find the airfield. As we approached the 'field, Frank really came to life and started barking orders. I did everything that he asked and then some. Soon we were on the ground and the aircraft rolled to a stop halfway down

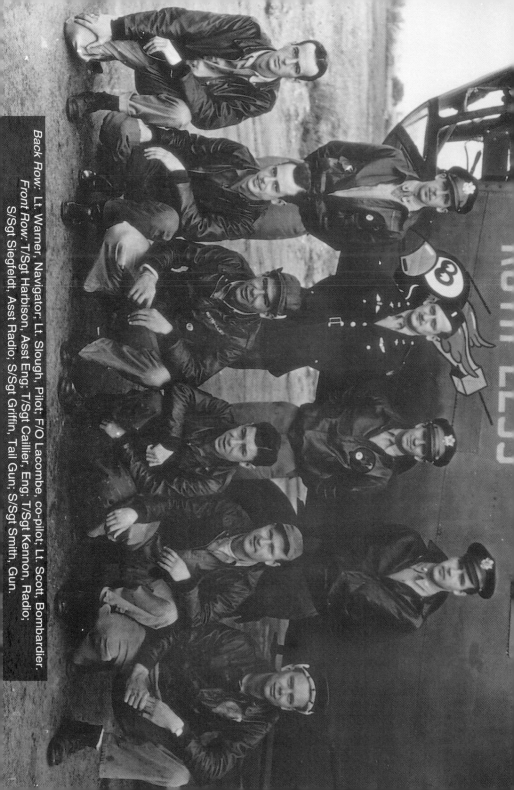

Back Row: Lt. Warner, Navigator; Lt. Slough, Pilot; F/O Lacombe, co-pilot; Lt. Scott, Bombardier.
Front Row: T/Sgt Harbison, Asst Eng; T/Sgt Caillier, Eng; T/Sgt Kennon, Radio;
S/Sgt Siegfeldt, Asst Radio; S/Sgt Griffin, Tail Gun; S/Sgt Smith, Gun.

the runway. I jumped out of the Liberator with all of my flying gear and ran towards the control tower. A Jeep met me about halfway, I told the Officer what had happened.

It was the first that they knew there had been an accident, as we had lost our radio in the crash and could not contact the base. The Officer whirled the Jeep around and streaked toward the Operations Building.

Soon a whole pack of people and equipment including doctors, were heading towards our B-24. The doctor went inside the ship to be with the Bombardier, while a rescue team on the outside cut him free. We were then taken to the Operations Building to recount what had happened. Afterwards, Frank and I were put aboard another Liberator and ordered to fly for two hours! When we got back, some of our crew who had bailed out were waiting for us.

All but one was found that day. The next day the missing crewman returned and we found that the Bombardier had suffered just a broken leg. The only other casualty on our crew was the Radio Operator, who had broken his ankle when he hit the ground.

Two days after the accident, some big shots from Consolidated Aircraft were brought in to examine the ship. They reported the aircraft so badly twisted that it was incapable of flying. They could hardly believe that we had flown it back after the collision. During this time I learned why Frank was cursing the Co-pilot. When the mid-air collision occurred he knocked everyone down on the flight deck in order to get out first. For that he was made a permanent IFC on kitchen police duties for the duration plus six months."

The local newspaper, The Pueblo Chieftain, reported the incident as follows:

"BOARD WILL INVESTIGATE BOMBER ACCIDENT"

"The missing crewman who had been missing for more than 24 hours after he had bailed out of a B-24 bomber near Manzanola yesterday after a mid-air collision, was found safe and unhurt today at a farmhouse in the region. He made his way to the house yesterday and spent the night there, being unable to reach a telephone until today.

Four of the airmen who jumped, were located within a short time of the accident. Prior to the discovery of the fifth man, aeroplanes from the Pueblo Army base, the La Junta base and the Pueblo civil air patrol, had flown repeatedly over the area near the crash, in an effort to locate him.

Searchers from the Pueblo base were on the ground all of last night and this morning. Bodies of the four Lieutenants and three Sergeants, who perished when their bomber crashed near the gunnery range, are in the Pueblo mortuary pending funeral arrangements. The accident occurred at 10.15 am Tuesday 23rd December 1942, when the two bombers were flying near to the gunnery range of the Pueblo air base, which is west of the bombing range. They were in formation on a routine flight, when one ship unexpectedly rose into the path of another.

The tail of the ill-fated craft was sheared off and the bomber plunged earthward before any of the seven crew in it could bail out. The B-24 burst into flames on striking the ground. Part of the tail of this ship was still on the front of the other bomber, when it made its way back to the Pueblo base".

1st lt. Frank Slough and Flight Engineer James E.Caillier, were the first 506 squadron crewmembers to receive the Distinguished Flying Cross in recognition of their bravery and heroism.

On the 17th January 1943, 506 sq. combat crews arrived at Salina in Kansas to collect their shiny new B-24's. Colonel Richard 'Dick' Butler was then a co-pilot on Walter Bunker's crew, he remembers Frank Slough and the trip over to England via the 'Southern Route':

Slough was a different kind of person. I believe he had been in the Royal Canadian Airforce, as he wore a pair of RCAF or RAF wings over his right breast pocket. I remember that he always had a very unkempt appearance.

He had long stringy blonde hair that usually hung down into his face. He had very bad teeth and his uniform usually looked like he had slept or flown in it, or both. But he was a very experienced and capable pilot, and people liked to fly with him.

We picked up our new aircraft including Slough's 'plane which he later christened 'Ruth-Less,' at Salina and left in a snow storm for De Ridder, Louisiana, as Morrison Field at West Palm Beach was too crowded to take us. We lost one aircraft and crew (Angel) on route to De Ridder. We were there a couple of days and then went to Morrison. We stayed at Morrison for a few days and then left on the 2nd February for Borinquen Field in Puerto Rico. We did not know what our final destination was to be, but suspected that we were going to Africa or India.

After several fun-filled days and nights we left for Atkinson Field, Georgetown, British Guyana and then on to Belem and Natal, Brazil. We were there a couple of days too before making a night flight across the Atlantic to Bathurst in British Gambia, landing there on a steel mat runway. We spent a couple of days there doing an engine inspection and living in horrible conditions. We were briefed to fly to Marrakesh, with a terrible warning of what would happen to us if we went down short of Marrakesh. The natives were far from friendly. We had an easy flight to Marrakesh and were there a few days staying in the best hotel in town, (I can still smell it!) and I can remember being served scrambled ostrich eggs for dinner!

It was here that we finally learned that we were going to England. We flew to St.Eval at Newquay, Cornwall. One night there, then on to Shipdham, Norfolk, arriving on the 23rd February. I think our flight was pretty typical of what all the 506th crews had experienced".

Dick Butler, 27th May 1995.

James Caillier comments on his experience of the trip via the Southern route with 'Ruth-Less' and his crew:

"After picking-up 'Ruth-Less' at Salina we flew to Fort Worth, Texas to collect some spare parts which had been lost when a B-24 crashed on take-off during the snow storm. In all we had enough spare parts loaded around the nosewheel for four 'planes.

We left for Louisiana staying over for one night, then proceeded to West Palm Beach in Florida where we spent four days getting drunk. Frank (Slough) got caught drinking with us enlisted men and the MP who captured us, put us back on our B-24 and told us to get the hell out of there. After that we flew to San Juan, Puerto Rico and shot a few coconuts out of the trees with a Thompson machine gun, then on to British Guyana for a night.

After leaving Belem we spotted a German U-boat at the mouth of the Amazon. Neither the German sub or we had any ammunition, but Frank dived our ship down towards the sub to give him a fright just for the hell of it. We crossed the Atlantic to Natal (*sic*) where we bought some bananas and oranges, which we thought might be useful in swapping for a little TLC in the UK. We had a very hairy landing at Bathurst, West Africa when we touched down on an improvised airstrip made with iron mats. Frank got real drunk after that! Next stop was Marrakesh, where we were stuck for thirty days waiting for a new supercharger regulator to be flown in from the US.We gambled with worthless French Francs and bought Arab eggs.

Newquay was our first taste of England, where a friendly barmaid in the local pub told me what a'sailor's dickie' was. As we flew over Shipdham and had our first glimpse of the new airbase, everyone yelled 'you'll be sorry'. After the Kiel raid when 'Ruth-Less' was shot up with 120 holes, we knew what they meant"

James Caillier, February 2000.

Harold Schwab who was destined to fly on 'Ruth-Less' for his last few missions, was not so lucky with his pilot Charles 'Whit' Whitlock. Schwab and the crew had been trained up on the B-24, but soon Lt.Whitlock received disheartening new orders. Their B-24 was taken from them and the crew was sent to Salina for a month of transitional B-17 training. Schwab was a tough cookie with a dry sense of humour having been brought up in the Bronx, New York and he soon got fed up with the gripers on the crew:

"If you don't like the transfer, go home to your mommies" he said stressing the word 'mommies'. Don Chase of the 44th B.G. continues the story:

"The transitional wasn't all that bad, we adjusted OK. In fact the 17's proved to be good ships but didn't have the speed, range nor bomb capacity of the B-24's, but they were readily manoeuvrable, reliable, airworthy craft. Their empennages at least, were sturdy, a feature that some early model B-24's lacked.

Checked out more or less in our B-17, we left Kansas for Prestwick, Scotland with a refuelling stop and weather briefing at Gander, Newfoundland, before crossing 'The Pond'. However, reports of heavy Atlantic weather and unfavourable winds kept us grounded for about two weeks. Finally we got the green light and headed east. The weather forecast had called for alto-cumulus clouds along our route, with tops at eight or nine thousand feet and with an assisting tail wind. Some three hundred miles out however, the clouds sloped upward.

We ascended lazily at first as if on a smooth riding escalator, twelve, fifteen, seventeen thousand feet. Then swelling cumulus popped through the level tops and light turbulence persuaded us to seek smoother air. To stay above the towering cumulonimbus clouds, we rose up through twenty-four thousand feet. No problem yet, even though we were heavy with various supplies. But still the non-forecasted clouds continued to fluff and mushroom up and the '17' climbed, twenty-six, twenty-eight, and the rolling cu's provided us with accompanying moderate turbulence, it was getting rough and major clouds lay ahead.

An adjacent '17' left our company nosing downward, then another, altogether we counted five of them. They disappeared into the undercast apparently heading for the deck. We reached the point of no return about the time we climbed to twenty-nine thousand feet in altitude. It was time of momentous decision for our pilot 'Whit'. Should we descend through the turbulence and embedded thunderstorms and take our chances of reaching Scotland with the other low-loaders, possibly wave hopping while fighting unpredicted headwinds? Stay on top? "Can we return to Gander?" 'Whit' asked the Radio operator if radio silence had been broken and if any pilots had indicated they were returning to Gander? None had. "Okay, we don't do either," 'Whit' said on the intercom, "We'll stay on top".

Lordy, just how high will this bird fly before her wings run out of support air? Oxygen, enough to get us through? Fuel enough? God it's cold. We've got to make it. These and other prayerful thoughts filled our minds and further chilled our bodies, sedentary to conserve oxygen. And still our '17' strained upward. "Pilot to crew", 'Whit' called on the intercom, "we're at thirty thousand one hundred and fifty feet, if our altimeter is correct. Oatmeal stick as high as she'll go . . . but we'll be OK". We prayed he was right.

Ahead and to the sides, flat topped anvils now crowned the cumulonimbus clouds. Some towered far above as we snaked around them. To the north and south other '17's' likewise avoided the higher thunderstorms cells. The '17's' looked like a disorganised flock of ducks preparing for a water landing, heads held high, outstretched wings canted into the horizon, tails low and dragging. Slowly the anvils dispersed. The mountainous clouds gradually relaxed and merged with the altos, allowing us to leave the tail-dragging heights for more tolerable altitudes. Our oxygen supply was depleted, but now we could breathe nature's oxygen.

Little more than fumes powered the engines as we entered Scottish airspace. After landing at Prestwick, we performed the half-serious, half-frivolous ritual of testing earth's solidity and affectionately patting the 'planes fuselage, a natural follow-up to the end of a scary flight.

Our '17' was like a giant friend incarnate, a beautiful high soaring, life saving sweetheart. Confidently we knew she'd carry us safely through our combat tour. No sir, average weighted B-24's would never have topped those clouds!

Unexpectedly our exuberance was short-lived. The first ominous news we heard was that only one of the low-roader 17's made it safely across the water. Apparently the other four in their battle against turbulence and head-winds, ran out of fuel before reaching Ireland or Scotland. A second blow assaulted us when we learned of our new orders: Leave the 17 at Prestwick, proceed to base at Shipdham and prepare to re-orient ourselves with the flight characteristics of the B-24.

Shafted again! Over the last two months we had gained confidence in the 17. We had rationalised her bomb-carrying and flight range limitations, coped with her all-electric systems, respected her sturdiness, and were at ease with her overall performance. 24's? They were like a long lost dream, a pleasant but fading memory.

It was bomb aimer Harold Schwab again – God rest his soul, unflappable, wry-humoured Schwab who arrested our mutinous stirrings. "Navigator" he addressed Robert Hicks, "Which way is west?" Hicks pointed. Deadpan and wordless, Schwab picked up his B4 bag and started to walk away. "Hey, where are you going Schwab?" someone asked. "Home" he answered, "I'm just not interested in this war anymore".

Chapter 3
LIFE AT
SHIPDHAM

SHIPDHAM was one of the many new bases constructed to accommodate the huge and mighty 8th USAAF. The airfield was built like most of the others to an RAF specification, using 550,000 square yards of concrete for the runways and hard standings, plus 37,000 square yards of tarmac were laid at a cost then of £1,100,000 to the British taxpayer.

Not only was Shipdham the first US heavy bomber base in Norfolk, Liberators operated out of there for longer than other Eighth Airforce combat airfield in Britain. Situated three miles south of East Dereham, the design of the airfield encompassed three intersecting runways, an encircling taxiway and thirty aircraft dispersal points. Three T2 hangars were grouped together adjacent to the technical site building on the south side of the fields, and the camp was dispersed among the fields and farms to the southeast. Accommodation for the 2,660 enlisted men and 460 officers, was constructed and there were storage tanks capable of holding 216,000 gallons of gasoline. When the USAAF took over the base, an additional twenty-five hard standings were constructed. Despite all of this, the US Corps of Engineers had to complete modifications to the runways and taxiways at Shipdham, by reinforcing then to withstand the weight of bomb-laden aeroplanes. To do this though, meant disturbing the ground immediately adjacent to the runways as the new topping was applied. The earth fill which was required to level the areas along the runways combined with heavy rain, caused

A bleak view of a squadron accommodation block at Shipdham.

prodigious amounts of mud to be produced around the Flight Line.

'Will' Lundy recollects:

> "Because transportation vehicles were in short supply, it was necessary to walk everywhere in the mess at least four times in a day. Because mud was found at all of the squadrons living quarters, Arctic or rubber overshoes were an absolute necessity whenever leaving the barracks, as the soil had not had time to settle following the construction work. Any vehicles which were available, were used to ferry combat personnel from their squadron sites, to and from briefing, or to and from their aeroplanes. Mostly Dodge weapon carriers were utilised, but occasionally the Jeeps were used, especially while the aircrews

DIAGRAM OF AIRFIELD

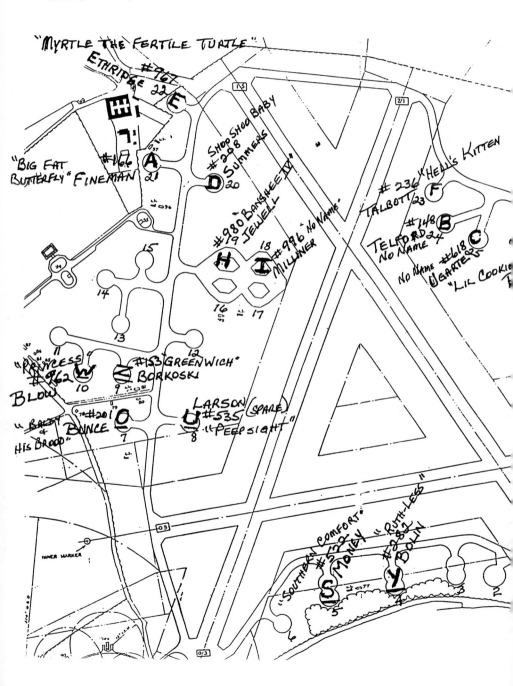

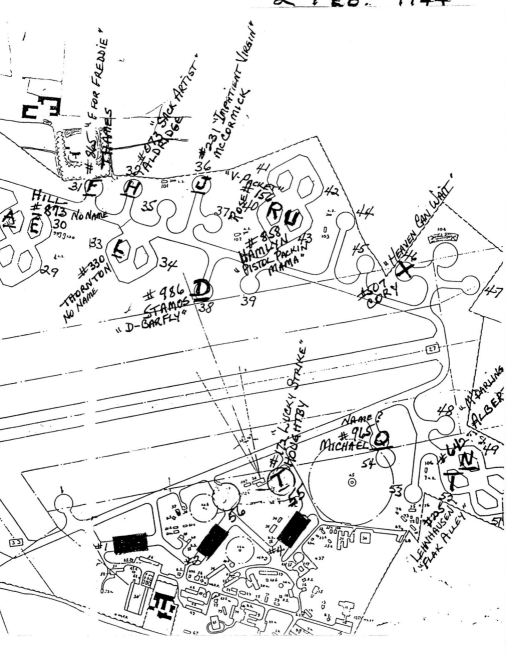

2 FEB. 1944

were flying, then the ground crews would shelter in the vehicles against the elements.

Ground crewmen sloshed and slid about in the mud, as they made their way out to the Flight Line for the pre-flight checks, virtually every morning and in complete darkness. Once the 'planes had departed, the ground crews would go back through the mud to their barracks to catch-up on some sleep. Around mid-day, it was back to the mess for lunch and then back out to the Flight Line, to await the returning 'planes. This was a nerve-racking time, as the ground crews awaited their respective charges.

As the aircraft returned, the rest of the day was spent filling the Liberators tanks with 100 plus octane gasoline, topping up the engine oil and other general maintenance chores. If the aircraft had been battle damaged, or had a more deep seated technical problem, the ground crews would trudge back to the mess for dinner, then return to the B-24 and work all night until she was once more serviceable. Repair work continued non-stop with the exception of meal breaks, until the aircraft was ready for further combat. Only then could the ground crew get their much needed rest."

The first winter at Shipdham was a very difficult and demanding time for the Americans. The gently undulating Norfolk countryside provided little natural shelter from the north and easterly winds. The only protection for the ground crews was the aircraft itself, and that had neither heating nor electric lights, except for the cockpit instruments. Therefore during the hours of darkness, maintenance work was carried out by flashlight alone and the same work could seldom be done wearing gloves. Much of the maintenance concerning engine nacelle or accessory sections, was bare handed in the freezing conditions. Eventually every dispersal point had it's own shelter for the ground crews, made out of materials commandeered from around the station. All the shelters had oil heaters and some even had a bed and mattress. The oil came from the Liberators engine sumps which were changed regularly, and when mixed with a little 100-octane gasoline, it burned beautifully in the artfully modified 30 or 50 gallon oil drums, which became the heaters.

The barracks themselves had single block walls and the roofs were corrugated asbestos. Little concern was paid to the heat retaining qualities of the structures which were very cold during the winter to live in. In the single large room which accommodated 30 to 45 men, there was in the centre of the building just a single, small coal burning heater. This would seem an obvious place to choose a bed, as near to the warmth as possible. But the heater was also the centre of most barrack room card schools and little sleep could be achieved if your bed was in the proximity of it.

'Ruth-Less' on her return from a mission at hardstand no: 4.

James Caillier recollects:

"Shipdham was a pretty boring place to be. I could not stand the beer hall but there were good movies and U.S.O.

A natural metal finish B-24H beating up the field at Shipdham.

shows. To cure the boredom I went to the dance hall in
Norwich as often as I could. We also had good poker
games during the day when we weren't flying.

Our crew was very close knit from the time of the mid-
air collision in Colorado and flying missions were so scary
that we were always on our toes. All the guys were a
wonderful bunch and we all trusted each other with our
lives. The whole crew looked up to Frank like he was a
dad because he was older than us and boy, he could really
fly. That made everything bearable and he treated us like
gentlemen. The rest of the squadron did not share the
same opinion of him, but that was because Frank did not
always press his uniform or shave, but we loved him. We
knew that 'Ruth-Less' would always get us there and back
with Slough at the controls, and we were very proud of

our B-24. I think everyone around Shipdham knew of 'Ruth-Less'. We made her known".

Frank Slough decided to call his Liberator 'Ruth-Less' after his wife Ruth, who he had left behind in the U.S. The 44th Bombardment Group dubbed themselves "The Flying Eightballs" with 506 squadron being the "Green Nosed Flying Eightballs".

Even before the arrival in the UK of the 44th Bombardment Group, it had become obvious that the Liberator, conceived in peacetime with little consideration for weather other than Californian blue skies, had many serious short-comings. So until modifications were corrected on the assembly lines, it was down to the hard-pressed ground crews at Shipdham to put things right. There were problems with the oxygen masks, which were of a crude design. The masks were connected to the aircraft's central oxygen supply line at a terminal and were vulnerable to mishaps. If the flexible quarter inch tube kinked at high altitude, unconsciousness or death would follow if not discovered quickly. Until new lubricating oil was developed, almost every B-24 machine gun would freeze inoperable in temperatures of minus 30 degrees Fahrenheit. During the winter, temperatures lower than minus 50F were common at altitudes of between 25,000 and 30,000 feet.

Endeavouring to prevent freeze-ups on those early missions, the guns were fired frequently in short bursts all the way to the target and back if the ammunition lasted. But even then, no matter how careful the gunners were, the guns would still freeze and aborts were common.

'Will' Lundy adds:

"Knowing that each abort weakened the effective force of those continuing on with the mission, aircraft in the 67th sq. and I believe all the 44th, soon started carrying 45 calibre Thompson sub-machine guns in the waist window area. This gun would operate in all temperatures, so we loaded it with tracers. If the regular guns froze, the waist gunners would take the sub-machine gun when any German fighters appeared and spray tracers towards it. Of course these tracers were not always successful."

31

Further problems encountered by the crew of 'Ruth-Less' and other B-24 crewmembers, were the difficulties found with the heated flying suits.

'Will' Lundy continues:

"Another 'accessory' problem was weather protection clothing. Until the improved electric heated suits arrived, flying in those woolly leather pants and jackets was downright miserable. Frostbite was all too common, with death from freezing always a distinct possibility. The four gunners in the rear section of the aircraft, were exposed to that terrible air whistling past them at 200 miles per hour. The chill factor must have been unbelievable. Those outfits were just great for us working on the B-24's, but unsatisfactory where the temperatures were so far below zero.

One cold afternoon, I was standing nearby as a combat crew was disembarking after a diversionary mission. Last to leave by the back hatch was Roy Klinger. I will never be able to forget the heart-rending scene, as that little tail gunner half-fell when he stepped onto the ground. He just stood there wavering as he fought to maintain his footage. He was a mess! His eyebrows and front hair were covered with white frost. Ice sheets covered the oxygen mask that he was fumbling to remove, and icicles hung down from that football-shaped gadget part of his mask and from his chin. The poor little guy was more dead than alive.

It seemed a long time before everyone realised his plight and leaped to help him. Damn! When will things start to get better? It would be many months more. All of this torture must be endured without even facing the enemy! And everyone knows the enemy is more than enough. These poor souls must endure it many times in aborts, recalls and diversions without one credit for a mission."

Similarly, the nerve centre of the aircraft, the flight deck or cockpit, was completely unprotected. Only thin plexiglass served as windshields and side windows, and the aluminium sheeting which formed the aircraft's skin provided little protection from flak, bullets or cannon fire. However the Liberators were eventually field modified with metal plating at strategic positions, to provide some defence to the crews from enemy fire.

Even though the ground crews had their discomforts, they did not compare to the problems of the aircrews. Here 'Will' Lundy describes an average winter's day at Shipdham, as a mission is prepared for:

"With a flash of the barrack lights and a sadistic 'gentleman' yelling "mission on", our day has begun. There is always the hope that it is a bad dream, but not this time, it's for real. A quick glance at my watch tells me it's 3:30am and I didn't get back from Norwich until after midnight. Oh well, what's a little sleep more or less.

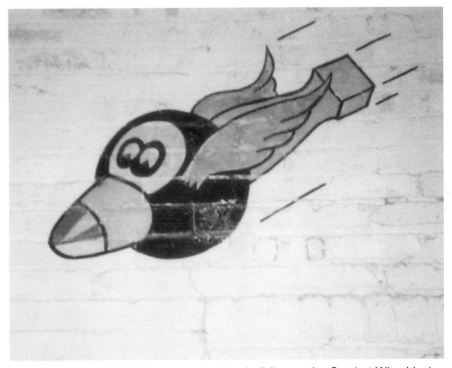

An example of 'wall art' surviving inside a building on the Combat Wing block at Shipdham. The 'Flying Eightball' was the symbol of the 44th Bombardment Group.

It was cold, very cold as I rolled over to quickly survey my work clothes. You must have a system like a fireman, everything going on in nothing flat. All around me in the large, one roomed barrack, about 35 aircraft maintenance men were too busily occupied with dressing, to grumble or complain. First things first, get your body weather-proofed! In a few minutes we are out into the inky black night, on our way for some coffee and a little food.

Site One is located near the centre of a large rectangle, with the longer parallel roads running north-south, connecting the hangar area to various sites. In daylight hours, the way to the mess hall requires the devious following of the road south, west, south, east and south again. A distance of nearly three-quarters of a mile. But under the cover of darkness we merely climb over a small

More surviving 'wall art'.

wire fence, follow a hedgerow, cross the street and sneak into the rear of the Communal Site. This path is taboo, as it supposedly would indicate to the enemy some activity. It never did. After a breakfast of powdered scrambled eggs, cold toast, washed down with scalding hot coffee from our metal GI cups, it's back out into that cold. Our job starts early, but just when did those cooks start? It seems they are in operation around the clock and do a damn good job of it, considering what they have to work with.

The jaunt over to our dispersal area must be at least five miles, so the four of us were especially grateful that we timed it right, for a passing truck headed for the motor pool picked us up. Those rubber goloshers keep the feet dry, but are a pain to hike in. But walk we must, around the hangars, eastward along the perimeter taxiway, around the bend and across the end of the main runway, then back west.

Finally there is our B-24 'Miss Diane', tucked away in a cul de sac back by another fence. To ready for pre-flight, it's up through the rear hatch, forward and open the bomb bay doors. Many times the armament men are ahead of us, loading bombs, installing guns and ammunition. Not this morning. Then up on to the wing and fuselage to remove the canvas covers. Have to do a balancing act up here, or find myself trying to keep from sliding off that frosty high wing.

No need to check the gas tanks as we just filled them a few hours ago, but did them anyway. Can't take a chance of anything which might jeopardise a mission. While I was performing my high wire act, the rest of the crew was going over 'Miss Diane' from stem to stern, all is in order.

George Baccash our Crew Chief climbed into the pilot's seat. I followed him into the co-pilots seat as Carl Stoddard and Bailey were pulling through the propellers, then becoming observers. Carl started the A.P.U. (Auxiliary Power Unit), a petrol driven generator that provided auxiliary power for instruments and starting the engines, lights etc.

No matter how many times I experienced it, the starting

and run-up of those engines always gives me a tremendous thrill. The feel of all that harnessed power at 50 inches of mercury is exhilarating. The four engines having successfully passed all instrument checks, we quickly shut down to conserve that precious blue 100+ octane gasoline. And with all other visual inspections completed, our immediate job was done. Now the waiting begins. There still is feverish activity all over the airfield. However as other pre-flights are progressing, minor repairs completed, bombs loaded etc. The sounds are all there, but nothing is visible except occasionally a momentary flash of light, as someone becomes careless with his torch.

Time drags on as we wait for daylight. There is no place to go to escape that bone-chilling dampness. The cold comes right through our fatigues, sweaters and jackets. So each of us in our own way tries to keep warm, either in the 'planes or out on the hard top, slapping his hands, jogging, but still shivering. Finally with the arrival of dawn come the power wagons, Jeeps and trucks bringing the combat crews. Our discomforts are forgotten. Now it's the business of getting the mission underway. The crew quickly unload their gear, verify and get everything in readiness, then join us in our huddle for small talk.

Time drags as the rising sun fought a losing battle with the thickening fog. The weather kept getting worse as did the temperament of us all. Time and again we've gotten this far, all set for take off and then had the mission scrubbed. So far this month we have had credit for two, maybe three missions and none since ten days ago. As we can only drop bombs on occupied countries when the targets are visible, chances of successful winter missions are rare.

There goes the red-red flare, mission scrubbed again, dammit! It's easy to feel sorry for yourself, so much wasted effort and needless suffering with the cold. But wait, think about those combat men. Think of the physical and mental anguish they must have suffered, thinking that this might be their last day on earth, the waiting, prepar-

36

ing yourself to face it, then nothing. My heart goes out to them, as they slowly reload the vehicles and leave. We have nothing to do now, but wrap up our 'planes and try to catch some sleep, and do it all over again tomorrow."

Will Lundy, May 1995.

'Will' Lundy (on right)

Chapter 4
'Ruth-Less'
Goes To War

ECHANICAL problems still dogged the 44th Bombardment Group and all had to be solved by study and
experiment. During the winter of 42/43 there were
troubles with the engines. This was caused by the pilots pulling back
the throttles to almost full extent at 25,000 feet, without using the
supercharger control. The improper engine performance was attri-
buted to the supercharger boost producing a lean fuel-air mixture.
Pilots were advised to open the throttles wide and to adjust the
manifold pressure with the supercharger controls. Another problem
affecting 'Ruth-Less' and other B-24D's, was the incorrect operation
of hydraulic supercharger regulators, which froze at altitude causing
congealing and irregular action. This finally resulted in the design of
an electronic regulator, which solved the problem

Original B-24's were painted a drab olive colour, with medium
green blotching on the wings and tailplane as camouflage. In 1942
and 1943, it was usual for a bomber crew to retain an aircraft for
most of their tour. Personalisation of each aircraft by their crews was
allowed, nicknames would be individualistic and the 'nose-art' was
often intricate and of a very high standard. Bomb symbols representing each credited mission, were painted vertically in yellow on
the camouflage. Surviving aircraft from the low level 'Ploesti'
mission code named "Operation Tidal Wave", would have a
horizontal bomb silhouette. As part of the 44th "Flying Eightballs",
'Ruth-Less' had a black eightball character with a nose, wings and

Bombardier Charlie Shaw (touching his hat)
with 'Ruth-Less' at the dispersal point.

bomb for a body. The colour green on the striped nose of the emblem signified 506 squadron, whilst the name 'eightballs' came from the black ball in the game of pool.

The first mission that 'Ruth-Less' was credited with, had Captain William N.Anderson at the controls on the 4th April 1943. Because this was a decoy diversion raid on the Dutch coast, a little duck was painted on the nose of 'Ruth-Less' to acknowledge that effort. Two further decoy diversion missions were flown, with Frank Slough back in the left-hand seat on the 1st of May 1943 to the Lizard Point area, then on the 4th May, 1st Lt. James McAtee flew her from Orford Ness to the North Foreland in Kent. In fact the 44th B.G. flew so many of these diversionary sweeps for the B-17 groups, that the Liberator crews began to call themselves the 'Second Bombardment Diversion Group'.

Ray Lacombe, co-pilot.

The four squadrons at Shipdham, the 66th, 67th, 68th and the 506th, each with nine Liberators, constituted the entire B-24 force in Europe available for daylight bombing in early 1943. The problems encountered with the differing performance of the B-17 and the B-24 aircraft was a headache. The B-24 had an optimum cruising speed some 20mph faster than the B-17. The Liberator was very difficult to fly in a tight formation, it was heavy on the controls and had an unnerving tendency to break away violently in the prop-wash or slipstream of another aircraft. The high aspect and wing loading of the 'Davis' wing, was the culprit for the Liberator's inherent instability and in the Eighth Air Force, the competence of a B-24 group came to be judged by how tight a formation they kept. The solution to most of these problems, was to place the Liberator formations to the rear of the B-17's and at a slightly different altitude.

The disastrous mission to Kiel on the 14th May 1943 will be forever etched in the memories of those in the 44th B.G. A change of tactics for the B-24 group, left them hopelessly exposed to enemy fire and the force suffered grievous losses. According to the Briefing Check Form for that mission which indicates the position of each

From left to right: , 'Chicken' Smith, 'Siggy' Seigfeldt and Elwood Harbison by 'Ruth-Less' at her dispersal point.

echelon in the formation, Frank Slough in 'Ruth-Less' was located in the second echelon from the front, on the far left hand side. Air Force strategies had ordered that the B-24's should be loaded with incendiary bombs, a weapon that had not been used for some months. The plan was, that flying low and holding back until the

Seigfeldt and Smith at their waist window positions inside 'Ruth-Less'.

hundred plus group of B-17's had dropped their 300 tons of H.E. (high explosives), the 44th would follow in to drop their incendiary's, which had a shorter trajectory than the regular ordinance.

Nineteen Liberators of the 66th, 67th and 506th squadrons departed Shipdham but soon encountered enemy fighters over the Dutch coast. Five of the B-24's were shot down before reaching the target, and another was lost on the return journey. Although reconnaissance photographs later showed the mission to have been a success, the three squadrons of the 44th had suffered a devastating blow. Some blame for the losses was levelled at the B-24 group flying a scattered formation, which left them vulnerable to enemy attack.

'Ruth-Less' and her crew were one of the few lucky aircraft that made it back, but she had taken more than her fair share of punishment, having been perforated by the scars of 125 flak and bullet holes. Sgt. James Caillier, the Flight Engineer on Slough's crew, wrote about that mission in a letter to Will Lundy in 1984:

"One experience I particularly remember is the trip back from Kiel. We had fought our way in and out against 124 German fighters and when we reached Shipdham, the control tower was only interested in whether our tyres were flat or not! They could see the holes in the ship and we reported no injuries. Our wheels were down and locked, but we couldn't give them the answer on the tyres.

Well, they sent us to Langford Lodge in Northern

'Chicken' Smith below his waist window position
(note the lucky seven on the dice artwork).

Radio Operator Dan Kennon poses by his girlfriend's name.

Ireland, which was an airfield set-up for heavy repairs and overhauls. They told us to try landing there and get the holes patched. Apparently it had taken the English engineers some time to build the runway at Shipdham, and they didn't want it to be all torn up by our B-24. We landed without any problem in Belfast (Langford Lodge Airfield), and it took a few days to get the holes patched, etc.

The only real problem came, when the tail gunner used the 'thunder mug' and forgot to put it under the bed at our accommodation. The ball gunner got his foot stuck in it! Our crew was very close, and the officers would often use our clothes so that they could go out with us. In fact that same trick almost got us into trouble in Florida and on our way overseas. But that's another story though".

Frank Slough seen climbing out of the bomb bay of 'Ruth-Less'.

Sgt Bud Johnson, the Crew Chief of 'Ruth-Less'.

Eventually the surviving crew members of the 44th B.G. received recognition for their bravery in the Kiel raid, when official order no: 40 dated the 29th November 1943 as decreed by Brigadier General Hodges, awarded the group the Presidential Unit Citation for:

"The successful fulfilment of this highly dangerous mission, which was due to the extraordinary courage, skill and devotion to duty of all concerned, and which will always be worthy of emulation. Such heroism reflects the greatest credit upon the 44th Bombardment Group (H), and its component squadrons and upon the United States Air Forces".

In March of 1943, Ray Lacombe transferred from the Royal Canadian Air Force to join the crew of 'Ruth-Less' as a co-pilot.

'Ruth-Less' was back in the air on the 17th May with 1st Lt. Walter Bunker and 2nd Lt. Dick Butler at the controls, flying a raid down to Bordeaux, France as part of a twenty-one aircraft B-24 group from the 44th, to bomb Nazi submarine pens and locks. Along with the 44th were eighteen Liberators from the 93rd Group, who had also flown to the Davidstowe Moor airfield near Camelford, Cornwall the day before to assemble for this mission.

To keep the Liberators beyond the range of German coastal radar, a 700-mile arcing course flown mostly at 2,500 feet was planned. Despite mechanical problems with the lead aircraft, precision navigation by the lead navigator in setting a new course within the curve of the original, ensured the B-24's simultaneously arrived over Bordeaux at 22,000 feet exactly on schedule. An accurate bomb release resulted in the harbour lock gates being shattered plus extensive damage to the port area and it's facilities.

Walter Bunker's own aircraft 'Earthquake McGoon', serial No: 41-24235, was still being repaired after receiving heavy damage in the Kiel raid. He and his crew were allocated 'Ruth-Less' again on the 29th May, to successfully bomb the docks and harbour installations at La Pallice in France.

No sooner had this mission been completed, that the Liberators of the 44th and other bombardment groups were withdrawn from the European Theatre of Operations (E.T.O). The rumour going around the bases, was that the high command had finally realised that the B-24 could not withstand the flak and the fighters of the enemy. There had been much acrimony and bitterness toward the B-17 groups, as the Liberator crews believed they were just being used as bait to draw German fighters from the Fortresses and the comment that the 'Flying Eightballs' in particular, were a jinxed outfit.

The truth was, that the Liberators were destined to attack one of the most strategically important and heavily defended targets in Europe.

Chapter 5

OPERATION 'TIDAL WAVE'. PLOESTI!

THE Liberator squadrons spent the early part of June 1943 practising low level flying. Modifications and other changes were made to the B-24D's. 'Ruth-Less' was equipped with a heavier nose armament and long-range bomb bay fuel tanks were fitted. The still secret Nordern bombsight was removed and in its place was installed a low-level type, which was in effect a modified gun sight. Each of the Liberators were minutely inspected and brought up to peak performance. The pilots and co-pilots seats were anchored to the floor by cables to prevent them being torn loose in case of a crash landing. Armour plating from wrecked German JU 88's was installed over the navigators table and under the pilot's seat for the protection of the pilots. A stationary gun was installed in the nose to be fired by the co-pilot by using a cable connected to the cockpit. With this arrangement the pilots had to point the nose of the aircraft at the ground gun emplacements to hit their target.

Frank Slough and his crew spent many hours flying 'Ruth-Less' at very low level, usually 150 to 300 feet, to practise bombing a specially allotted target in the Wash. There was much speculation amongst the squadron personnel as to the purpose of this training.

In the last week of June, official orders sent the Liberator groups to North Africa via Portreath, on a temporary posting of the task force to Benina Main near Benghazi in Libya. 'Ruth-Less' departed Portreath on the evening of the 27th June on her journey to the heat and dust of a Libyan summer in the desert. On their arrival it soon became apparent as to the target for which they had been conducting their low-level training.

Ploesti had a complex of refineries and storage facilities adjacent to the Rumanian oilfields, which could not be reached from bases in England as a return trip. However from North Africa via the backdoor, it was just within range. Strategists deduced that the destruction of the refineries, where Hitler was currently receiving up to 60% of his fuel requirements, would have a dramatic effect on the Nazi's ability to wage war and may even shorten the duration of it. The Germans had no oil resources of their own, apart from a limited synthetic oil production capability. Therefore Hitler needed quick victories, hence the Bliztkrieg type offensives which were initially so successful.

It was the Russians who first realised the value of the Rumanian

'Ruth-Less' out in the desert at Benina Main. 'Audrey' was obviously the girlfriend of original Bombardier Lt Scott who had since transferred to another crew.

oilfields to the Germans, and bombed them within 36 hours of being invaded during the Nazi offensive, code named "Operation Barbarossa". The Americans first attacked Ploesti in June 1942 causing little damage, but this effort merely resulted in the Germans beefing up defences around the oil installations.

Herb Clough, crew chief (on right) and Al Orr, assistant crew chief.

The Ploesti raid did not occur immediately, as the bombers were required to give some assistance to the code named T.O.R.C.H. Allied invasion of Sicily and Italy under the code name of "Operation Husky". Slough piloted 'Ruth-Less' on her first mission from Benina, to strike at the railway marshalling yards at Messina, Sicily on the 5th July. The next day 'Ruth-Less' attacked the Gerbini aerodrome in Italy. Slough soon found the enemy just as hostile in this part of the world too and flying without fighter protection was especially uncomfortable.

1st Lt. Horace Austin was assigned 'Ruth-Less' and two of Slough's crewmembers, navigator George Grimes and radio operator Dan Kennon, for two missions to bomb targets at Catania, Sicily. The first on the 8th July was to bomb a communications centre, but because of numerous technical problems with the aircraft, no: 2 generator U/S, rear turret U/S, feed boosters motor top turret U/S and acid loss from one battery, Austin aborted the mission and returned with his 12 X 500lb bombs.

Elwood Harbison, the Top Turret Gunner.

Better luck prevailed for Austin on the 10th July, when railway marshalling yards were bombed. The Sortie Report completed after this mission has the following information:

51

Time Up 12.20 Time Down 19.20 Total Time 07.00

Base of clouds 15,000 - 20,000

Visibility: Good, 15 - 18 miles

'Siggy' SEIGFELDT at his right waist window gun position.
'Kitty' was his girlfriend back in the US.

Took off #4 position, #2 element, #2 flight. Reached altitude of 24,000 feet at 15.05 hours. In #2 position, #1 element, #2 flight at target. Made a 60-second run at 40 degrees, dropping 12 X 500 lb. American GP in train, at 60-foot intervals. Observed bombs to fall at M19. Observed other bombs to hit at M27, IM 17 - 19. Observed large fire and white smoke at WX 7.

Frank Slough on right of picture with Ray Lacombe.

Observed B-24 #4 engine smoking, losing altitude and going south, southeast.

AA - Heavy calibre, light intensity, aimed and accurate. Subject to AA at bombing point and two minutes after run.

Fighters - nil.

Damage - nil.

Mechanical difficulties - IFF blew up, waist gun noisy, radio screwed up.

Observed large fire and black at Cape Santa Croce and much black (smoke) at Messina.

Slough was in command of his ship again for three more missions to Italy on the 12th, 13th and 15th July, when the targets were railway marshalling yards at Reggio Di Calabria, Cretone aerodrome and the airfield at Foggia. Y-282 visited the railway marshalling yards at Naples on the 17th July under the command of 1st Lt.

Stevens and then Slough took 'Ruth-Less' to Rome on the 19th, where the Littorio marshalling yards were blasted.

The 1st August 1943, is another important date to go down in the annals of the 44th BG's history, as this was the day Ploesti was attacked, in this famous or infamous mission. The Ploesti raid has since been called a "20th century Charge of the Light Brigade", such was the prospect of survival. The round trip to the target entailed a distance of around 2,700 miles, much of it over hostile enemy territory. Before the raid Major General Brereton, the commander of the 9th Air Force and architect of the mission said:

"We expect our losses to be 50%, but even though we should lose everything we've sent but hit the target, it will be well worth it".

Brereton managed to convince General Eisenhower to give his

Navigator George Grimes checking his map of North Africa.
He was later killed in action with another crew.

support to the raid. Eisenhower was initially very sceptical of the alleged benefits of such a mission and was reluctant to release the bombers from the support of the Allied advance into Italy.

Ground crews had their work cut out, preparing the aircraft for this vital mission, but were hampered by the hot, dry and dusty conditions. One of the main problems was the dust and sand, which continually played havoc with the engines by blowing into the air intakes. The engineering section had to solve these problems by initiative and improvisation. Ground operating of the engines was kept to a minimum and dust excluders were fitted to them when the aircraft were parked.

There was a critical shortage of spare parts, which necessitated the cannibalisation of unserviceable aircraft to keep the others flying. Another problem was the desert heat damaging the fuel cells in the

View of front left-hand side of 'Ruth-Less'. The Flying Eightball logo was erased for security reasons, prior to the aircraft's departure for Africa.

Liberator's wings, causing them to leak. It was very difficult locating the leaks as the green dye, which showed on the wing when a leak occurred, coloured a whole area of the wing and never revealed distinctly the proper cell which was leaking. With the aid of inspection plates and good guesswork, the crew chiefs generally found the correct cell on the first attempt.

In a pre-mission address to all the bomber crews, General Brereton told them that this raid would be the 'final knockout blow' to the Germans and could win the war. Unfortunately he omitted to inform the airmen of German developments around Ploesti, such as their deployment of 125 fighters into the immediate area and the steady strengthening of defences around the oilfields and refineries

Bombardier Charles Shaw. He too was later killed in action after transferring to another crew.

Colonel Leon Johnson, on right, shaking hands with General Ent.

Aerial view of the cracking plant at Ploesti.

A Liberator escaping from the fiery inferno.

The scene of devastation at Ploesti.

over recent months. The German ME 109 units comprised of 1/JG4 led by Hans (Hasi) Hahn and IV/JG27 commanded by Lieutenant Burk. Also pilots of the Rumanian Air Force flying ME 109's and bizarrely, British made Gloster Gladiator biplanes, would assist their Luftwaffe colleagues in the defence of Ploesti.

Things started to go wrong from the outset. Several Liberators crashed on take off, including one containing a lead navigator. Altogether eleven B-24's did not make the mission through technical problems or accidents.

'Ruth-Less' flying with the 44th Group led by Colonel Leon Johnson in his B-24 'Suzi-Q', departed Benina Main at 05.00 hours. They flew across the Mediterranean and over Corfu, Later skimming over the lush fields and pastures of the Balkans, both the 44th and 98th formations reached the correct I.P. (Initial Point) at Floresti, for the southwards turn to their targets.

Heavy flak over the occupied territory caused confusion and one group of Liberators made a wrong turn towards Bucharest. Radio silence was broken when the Americans realised their mistake and this alerted the Germans well before they reached the target. One of the main factors of this mission was the element of surprise, this was now lost and would cost the airmen dear, as the Germans had enough time to get their fighters airborne and ready for the assault. Over Bulgaria, clouds caused the B-24 formations to break up and the bombing elements became widely separated.

'Ruth-Less' was in a 'follow up' group and among the last aircraft to attack the refineries. The flak batteries were waiting for them. Slough held her steady as his bombardier 1st Lt. Charles Shaw, prepared to release their bombs. Only 6 X 500lb were loaded, to allow a greater uplift of fuel. They were toggled in train at 25-foot intervals and were fitted with 45-second delay action fuses in order to allow the Liberators to get away before they exploded. This plan backfired as some B-24's were brought down as the bombs dropped from previous aircraft exploded underneath.

Slough pushed his attack home and descended Y-282 into the nightmare of the fiery and smoke-filled inferno; the refinery was literally blowing up in his face. 'Ruth-Less' was subjected to intense light flak and ground arms fire, two minutes before and two minutes after the target was hit. Flames from parts of the refinery such as the cracking plant, were shooting over three hundred feet

Ploesti ablaze. This photograph was taken by the tail gunner on 'Ruth-Less'.

into the air as 'Ruth-Less', severely buffeted by the hot updraughts continued her run. There were explosions going off all round as Slough, having heard from Lt. Shaw that the bombs had been released, shoved the throttles forward to full power and swooped the aircraft through an adjoining wheat field, as they made their escape.

James Caillier recalls the action:

"As we were the last ship over the target, we saw our bombs bounce on the roadway and go right through the walls of the cracking plant. They were delayed action fuses on those bombs, and some from previous aircraft were still going off as we flew through the smoke and flames. There were a lot of people gathered around the refinery perimeter. I particularly recall seeing a lady wearing a red dress. She seemed so out of place that I didn't fire again, because I was concerned that I might hit her or one of the other civilians.

The next thing I saw were huge fireballs blazing on the ground. We figured out they were B-24's that had crashed and rolled. 'Ruth-Less' had taken a hit from a 20mm on number one engine. The parts, which hold the propeller blades together, were damaged. Slough asked what setting we could use on the superchargers and still be safe. They are redlined at 50 inches of mercury, so we discussed the problem and decided to set them at 45 inches.

Frank took us so low as we left the target that we had to hedge hop as we had a fighter chasing us. After jumping one hedge I shot the Messerschmitt down and we were credited with that kill. Fortunately we were only hit once and made it back to Benghazi.

After that we were put in Purple Heart corner for 15 missions and sent to the 'Flak Shack' for a little R & R. Frank had a nice room at the Magreb Hotel in Benina and we were always welcome to visit him. He got a bit upset one day though, when he discovered that we had mistaken his foot bath for a urinal".

The Americans made their escape, but German ME 109E and ME 110 fighters pursued the Liberators from the target. A desperate air battle now followed as the unleashed German fighters pressed home their attacks. The crew on 'Ruth-Less' let rip with all they had, as 30 to 35 fighters working in pairs, took their revenge. Sgt. James Caillier the flight engineer firing from the left waist gun position, shot down one of the ME 109's and it was seen to crash by Sgt's E. W.Harbison and H. Siegfeldt. Sgt. Harbison in the top turret position, also hit another ME 109 which caught fire and crashed, as observed by tail gunner Robert Griffin and navigator George Grimes. The crew of 'Ruth-Less' were duly credited with both of these 'kills' and the appropriate swastikas were painted on the nose of Y-282 as confirmation.

Slough eased 'Ruth-Less' back onto the runway at Benina, the time now being 17.37, over twelve and half-hours airborne. As the crew clambered out of the hatches and jumped down, a quick survey of the battle damage revealed the shot-up cowling on no: 1 engine. One of the crew shouted to the others to look underneath the aircraft. An inspection of the belly found dozens of wheatstalks attached to the underside. Slough had cut a swathe through that wheat field just inches above the ground at nearly 300 mph. 'Ruth-Less' had surely been put through her paces that day.

The mission although boldly conceived, had been poorly organised. The plan was that the lead aircraft would navigate for all the rest. Unfortunately as these lead ships were shot down, the crews following behind found themselves deep in enemy territory without the knowledge of how they could find their way out. On their return, the surviving aircraft who struggled back from this terrible ordeal, had only one thing in mind as their fuel reserves dwindled . . . to get their aircraft back on the ground anywhere in friendly territory.

At Pachino in Sicily, the RAF was operating Spitfires out of a small dust strip. On the day of the Ploesti raid, to the disbelief of the RAF ground personnel there, they saw a Liberator lining up to land. Coming in at 140mph, the 35 ton Liberator would never stop before the end of the runway, and sure enough in a huge cloud of red Pachino dust, the B-24 careered off the end of the runway and ploughed into a vineyard. Shortly after other Liberators were on their final approach, sometimes coming in from both ends of the runway, but fortunately not simultaneously. Each subsequent landing was even more crazy and spectacular than the last, as the pilots violently manoeuvred to avoid the other aircraft, most of which lay in rather undignified positions, some on their wing tips or others with their undercarriage collapsed.

Soon there was a long elliptical line of Liberators deep into the vineyard, many of which were badly shot up. Men from the RAF medical unit raced to help the wounded American aviators. Those who had not suffered physical harm had evidently been subjected to excessive and exceptional mental strain. They hugged each other, some kissed the ground, while others filled their pockets with the red Pachino dust, such was their joy that they had survived.

In all, 54 of the 177 B-24's that had participated in the mission were lost, along with 532 airmen. Eight crews were interned in Turkey when critically short of fuel, they diverted and landed there. Though the attack effectively knocked out about 40% of Ploesti's refining capacity, the oil complex was only operating at 60% of capacity at the time of the attack. The Germans easily made up the shortfall and the installations were fully operational again within a few months.

After the war Marshall of the RAF, Sir Arthur 'Bomber' Harris, commented in his memoirs on the worthiness of attacking 'panacea' targets such as the oil refineries at Ploesti. He questioned the use of many squadrons of American bombers diverted from the main offensive against German industry for long periods, with crews trained just for one spectacular low level attack, that could not be followed up, and which had little lasting effect on the deliveries of Rumanian oil products to Germany. He states that:

'The loss of these squadrons for many months materially reduced the American build up for the main offensive against Germany itself'.

For their part, American Generals like Spaatz and Eaker thought that Harris was 'all washed up' in his conviction that the carpet bombing of German cities, would hasten the collapse of the Nazi economy, demoralise the German people, and negate their enthusiasm to further pursue the war. The Americans believed in bombing specific strategic targets rather than the destruction of population centres like Hamburg and Dresden, although they did also participate in these raids. Ploesti epitomised the radically different concepts of the Allies respective bombing strategies.

The refineries at Ploesti were not attacked again until April 1944.

Because Ploesti was the scene of many individual acts of heroism and bravery, the unprecedented award of five Medals of Honour for a single operation were presented, four of which went to 8th Air Force personnel. The 44th B.G. commander Leon Johnson, received his on the 23rd November 1943 in a parade in front of Shipdham's control tower, with the surviving crews who participated in the raid.

Once again, 'Ruth-Less' had survived against all the odds, bringing her crew safely home. She must indeed be a lucky ship.

Since the 7th August, it had been planned that all the B-24 groups would initiate another long range and arduous mission, to hit the Messerschmitt ME109 production lines at the factory situated in Wiener-Neustadt, Austria. This target was again at the extreme edge of the B-24's flight time endurance, but the element of surprise by taking this route would stack the odds in the Americans favour.

1st Lt. Horace Austin was in the hot seat again as he flew 'Ruth-Less' off from Benina at 07.00 hours on the 13th August. The 12-hour mission required careful planning and accurate navigation. Even with the addition of bomb bay tanks, it was not considered prudent for the B-24's to return to their Libyan bases, but instead would make for the nearer Tunisian airfields. In all 'Ruth-Less' and the other Liberators met little opposition during the mission, except for a Staffel of FW 190's over Austria and another of ME 109's on the return over Southern Italy. At the target, only a token resistance of accurate anti-aircraft fire was encountered. Two of the four ME 109 assembly shops were severely damaged, reducing production from 270 fighters in July to 184 in August.

The return of the Liberators to their bases in England was further delayed, due to the requirement to assist the final Allied advance in Sicily. Slough and his crew flew three more missions bombing Italy on the 21st, 24th and 25th August respectively. The targets were the Leghorn docks and harbour installations, railway marshalling yards and warehouses at Pisa, and then Pisa again to attack the Lucca aerodrome although this mission was subsequently recalled.

Colonel Leon Johnson, commander of the 44th B.G. Shipdham, after receiving
the Medal of Honour for the Ploesti raid on the 23rd November 1943.

Medal of Honour parade. Officers of the 44th B.G. that participated in the Ploesti mission are inspected by: (from left to right) Gen. Posey, Gen. Eaker, Col. Johnson, and Gen. Devers; (from right to left) Lt. Ray Lacombe and Lt. George Grimes.

General Devers making his address to the men, Medal of Honour day.

Officers awaiting inspection, Medal of Honour day. Lt. Charles Shaw is second from the right, Ray Lacombe fourth and George Grimes fifth.

Colonel Leon Johnson of Moline, Kansas, standing in front of Ploesti survivors, Medal of Honour day.

Medal of Honour parade. Photograph taken from the control tower.

Chapter 6

BACK AT SHIPDHAM

BACK at base, 'Ruth-Less' underwent an extensive overhaul, one engine was replaced and a great many malfunctioning parts were changed. Ray Lacombe was transferred to the 67th squadron and given his own crew after being promoted to the left seat. On the 6th September, Slough flew Y-282 on a North Sea diversion for the infamous Stuttgart mission as part of four B-24 groups. The 9th saw 'Ruth-Less' striking the Luftwaffe airfield at Abbeville, France in a S.T.A.R.K.E.Y. deception raid, while other aircraft hit a convoy of ships which were sighted off Texel. The following day Slough was airborne again with Y-282, but the squadron was recalled due to bad weather.

A mission to the Luftwaffe aerodrome at Chartres on the 15th September included the novelty of a late take off and a return for a night-time landing. The German held airfield was successfully hit, but night fighters shot down one Liberator as they intercepted the group. Apparently on return to Shipdham there was some difficulty, as night-time landing procedures were not correctly followed, all the B-24's did make a safe landing eventually. There is quite a gap now before 'Ruth-Less' is flown on another mission.

On the 18th October Slough and his crew flew a decoy diversion over the North Sea, with the additional bonus of a sortie credit for that one. Apart from that, Y-282 only flew training missions between the 15th and 18th October. Sometime towards the end of October, the Slough crew were broken up with James Caillier, 'Siggy'

James Caillier (laying down) looking very relaxed with his new crew on 'The Impatient Virgin'. Also with him from the original 'Ruth-Less' crew are Seigfeldt and Griffin.

Ray Lacombe and the crew of 'Peep Sight'.

Siegfeldt and Griffin finishing their tour with the crew of the Liberator 'The Impatient Virgin'.

Due to poor weather, a mission was cancelled on the 6th November, but on the 13th 1st Lt. Wayne Middleton and his crew were assigned 'Ruth-Less' for a raid on Bremen. Frank Slough flew this mission in another aircraft as the Lead Pilot for the group. It was a damp and overcast day typical of the time of year. Seven of the

Ray Lacombe and the crew of 'Sack Artists'. The crew bailed out over Switzerland on the 18th March 1944 and were interned.

escorting P38 fighters were forced to withdraw, due to a combination of the severe freezing temperatures at flight level, which caused mechanical problems, plus the tenacious resistance of the enemy fighters.

Ray Marner a crewmember who flew that mission wrote:

Pilot Dick Butler (with his back to the camera) with the crew of 'Earthquake Mc Goon'. Dick flew 'Ruth-Less' on a couple of occasions.

General Devers and Colonel Johnson inspect a Liberator at Shipdham.

"We went over Bremen today and everything went wrong. The mission was unsuccessful and the 44th lost quite a few ships. One of ours circled around the field and then cracked-up (crashed) a few miles away. A kid named Olsen was killed and also Cliff Hurst. I knew Hurst very well. Ralph Strait isn't expected to live through the night. Two others will probably die. They asked all men with blood type AB to report to the hospital. Hamel and Fleming (Bill Strong's crew) completed their 25th mission. They will go home soon."

(AUTHORS NOTE: Ralph Strait did survive and subsequently joined the Bolin crew flying 'Ruth-Less' early in the New Year).

Another veteran Liberator. Note how the 'Flying Eightball' logo has been masked off for this publicity shot.

On the 16th November 1943, poor weather over the usual targets in Germany and France led to an interesting change of destination for Y-282, when 1st Lt. Johnson and his crew undertook a mission to Rjukan, Norway. Here an electricity generating plant was hit due to the belief that it was associated with heavy water production allied to German nuclear experiments. Further good weather over Norway on the 18th entailed a return visit for 'Ruth-Less' with 1st Lt. Wayne Middleton back at the controls, when a German aircraft repair depot at the Kjeller airfield near Oslo was bombed.

Elwood Harbison (second from left) and James Caillier (third from right) survived their tour of 25 missions and became gunnery instructors at Shipdham.

Once again 'Ruth-Less' was lucky. Bombing from a height of 12,000 feet, the group of nearly one hundred aircraft turned for home, when they were set upon by a Staffel of ME 109's and a few

JU 88's. Altogether six B-24's were shot down and three others, which were badly damaged, limped to the safety of Sweden where the aircraft and their crews were interned.

Lt. Middleton flew Y-282 again on the 26th November when a Focke-Wulf aircraft factory and submarine pens were struck at Bremen. The 11th December saw Middleton and 'Ruth-Less' reunited for a trip to Emden in Germany, to destroy a transportation centre there. 1st Lt. Johnson took 'Ruth-Less' back to Kiel on the 13th to bomb shipbuilding and submarine yards, nearly seven months to the day since her last tough mission there. Two more trips to Bremen on the 16th and 20th with pilots Johnson and Middleton completed Y-282's official missions for that year. Good fighter support, despite the high winds and poor weather, meant that losses were kept to a minimum on both of those sorties.

As the New Year approached, there was increasing concern expressed by the British government regarding reports of huge concrete structures being built in the Pas de Calais region of France. It had become known that the Germans had a programme of secret weapons manufacture and Allied intelligence had identified the assembly and storage sites for the launching of V1 'Doodle-Bug' flying bombs. Altogether nearly seventy targets were recognised in the Pas de Calais area and were given the codeword 'NOBALL', the operation to destroy them was dubbed 'CROSSBOW'.

'Ruth-Less' did not fly another mission until the 14th January 1944, when she attacked a NOBALL site whilst piloted by 1st. Lt. Sayer. On this trip the 506th Squadron led the 67th Sq. from Shipdham to bomb military installations at Ecalles Sur Buchy, France. Captain James McAtee was the Command Pilot. Of the nine B-24's that departed base, one returned early due to technical problems. Altogether the Group, with reportedly excellent results, dropped 95 X 500 lb G.P. (General Purpose) bombs.

Chapter Seven

THE BOLIN CREW FLY
'RUTH-LESS'

THE Bolin crew came together as a result of squadron politics and misfortune. This is not the best way for a crew to start fighting a war, add a few strong personalities and you have a

James Bolin on the day he graduated from college

James Bolin's wife Betty and son Michael.

recipe for trouble, or at least discontentment. Being a 'make-up' crew cobbled together, with your senior officer an unknown quantity from another squadron, can have an unsettling effect on a group of men, trained to work as a cohesive fighting unit.

1st Lt. James Ogden Bolin was born on the 16th May 1919 in Pine Bluff, Arkansas. He had four brothers and a sister. 'Oggie' as he was nicknamed, played Halfback for the Arkansas Democrat All-State High School Football team, otherwise known as the 'Zebras' by the age of seventeen. He was a very fit and athletic young man with a height of 5:10 and weighing 170 pounds, according to a newspaper report on the team. On the 11th January 1938, his popularity amongst his peers was confirmed when the Freshman Class elected 'Oggie' president of the Student Senate at the University of Arkansas. After the meeting Bolin said that he appreciated:- "The great signal that the Senior Class gave me by electing me President of the Class of '38. I am sure with the co-operation of the student body, this year will be one of the most successful."

In 1937, 'Oggie' ended his high school gridiron career in a blaze of glory, scoring the seven points that beat the Zebra's ancient rivals, the Little Rock Tigers, seven to six. He caught a long pass for the touchdown and calmly kicked the extra point, which spelled defeat for the Tigers. As a symbol of his great performance during the season, he was named 'Quarterback of the All-Conference Eleven'.

Bolin accepted an athletic scholarship to the University of Arkansas and in his junior year volunteered for the Army Air Force, leaving the campus in November 1940. He finished his primary flight training at Spartan Flying Field, Muskogee, Oklahoma, only after winning a terrific battle with pneumonia in the final weeks of his training. From Muskogee he was sent to Randolph Field, San Antonio, Texas to complete his Army Air Corps work where he was also promoted to Top Sergeant. He received his wings and commission in July 1941, at Kelly Field, Texas. On his graduation day, he married Betty Welch of Joplin, Missouri and from that union a son, Bryan Michael, was born in 1942.

Bolin, serial number 0424895, first flew twin engine B-25 Mitchell aircraft, then he and his squadron in January 1943 began transitional training at Langley Field, Virginia onto B-24's for anti-submarine work. 2nd Lt. Art Grimes graduated from navigation training at Hondo, Texas on the 8th May 1943. James Bolin had asked for Grimes to be assigned to his crew, which was just being assembled. Art Grimes writes:

"We had the newest B-24 equipped with radar and we were moved around the various coastal areas of the Atlantic and Gulf Coasts in the USA, as (German) sub- marine were reported. Towards the end of July '43, our crew was alerted for immediate transfer to England, to replace a crew that had been lost in combat. We were sent to Langley Field to pick up another new B-24 with the latest radar and long-range bomb bay fuel tanks for twelve-hour patrols. We flew the 'plane to a base at Dunkeswell near Exeter, Devon where we joined an

American anti-submarine squadron attached to RAF Coastal Command.

We immediately started flying the long anti-submarine patrols and flew virtually every other day. We sank a German U-boat on one of our last patrols in early September. Unfortunately our squadron was disbanded later that month, as the US Navy was assigned all anti-submarine patrol activities as of the 1st October 1943.

Crews who had in excess of 400 hours flying the Bay of Biscay patrols, were returned to the US for strategic bombing training and further assignment to the Pacific Theatre. A few of the newer crews did not meet the time criteria and the likes of us were posted to the 8th Air Force. Our crew was assigned to the 66th squadron, 44th Bombardment Group at Shipdham. We received some training for combat bombing missions and were given our first mission to Knaben-Kjeller in Norway on the 16th November, to bomb the molybdenum mines there. Shortly after leaving Shipdham, we experienced problems with our no: 3 engine over the coast, and Bolin stated that because it was such a long flight, we would not be able to complete the mission on the remaining three engines, so he opted to abort."

Art Grimes, January 1995.

Merrill Berthrong remembers 'Oggie' Bolin well, he joined the crew at Langley Field as the co-pilot:

"He (Bolin) was a free spirit and contemptuous of military authority. He delighted in bending the rules and we got along well, as I also was not one to enjoy the 'military regime'. 'Oggie' always strove to excel – to fight to win. During the many hours of boredom we would play gin rummy and I would invariably win, which annoyed him excessively. He did not mind the amount of money he lost, he just hated losing. He never talked of private matters, his family or things of a personal nature.

He loved to fly and was a superb pilot. 'Oggie' had been a flight instructor early on and was an excellent tutor.

Our first assignment with anti-submarine patrols was on B-25's, which were new to me. He insisted on checking me out personally and we spent hours shooting landings. I had a great confidence in his skills as a pilot. I recall once when we were stationed at Virginia, we were sent with our B-24 to participate in a rally at Cambridge, Massachusetts and were allowed to fly low over the parade. I telephoned my parents to look out for me, as this was my hometown.

At roof top height I said to 'Oggie', "let me fly it over my house". He replied "sure" and we did. Afterwards he said "do you call that a 'buzz-job'? Let me show you". So he took over and brought the 'plane so low, I was sure he would blow the tiles off the roof - it took my breath away.

My most memorable flight with 'Oggie' was an anti-submarine patrol over the Bay of Biscay. We were circling a fishing boat that wasn't supposed to be there and trying to decide what to do, when a JU88 flew out of the clouds and shot out two engines on the same side. He made two passes as our gunners returned fire. We dropped our depth charges and threw out all other loose equipment to lose weight as the aircraft struggled for altitude. It took both of us pilots applying full rudder to steer a straight course. We radioed our position and the British sent some fighters to protect us and escort us back to a base in Southern England.

Once we were with the 66th squadron at Shipdham, because of the maximum effort policy and the high combat losses at the time, we were sent on combat missions almost immediately. We had no training in high altitude formation flying and had great difficulty adjusting. 'Oggie' did not have much experience in formation flying and was exceedingly frustrated when he did not do it well. In exasperation he would turn the controls over to me and would get even more irritated when I did it better than he from the 'wrong' seat".

Merrill G. Berthrong, July 1995.

Bolin wrote a letter to his family of his experience flying to the UK and the incident over the Bay of Biscay:

Dear Woody, Doty and Larry,   11TH AUGUST 1943

I received your two letters yesterday and enjoyed them immensely. As you probably know, mail from home is looked forward to with great zest and is just about the best morale builder available. Yours was the first bit of news I've heard from home since I left - yours and the letter Sis wrote which I received at the same time.

To begin with, our trip over was a nightmare. We were on instruments in icing conditions practically all the time and it was at night, which made matters worse. Everything on the ship iced up including our radio antenna, and we were out in the middle of the Atlantic Ocean, with no contact with the outside world. Then our lights went out and I was flying instruments by flashlight, when our air speed indicator suddenly disappeared below stalling. After diving the ship momentarily and not picking up any more speed, I realised that our pitot tube was frozen. The gremlins were really working on us and such hectic incidents such as these occurred all through the night.

When dawn finally came, we discovered that the wings were well iced up and that our gasoline was low because we had been carrying all that extra weight. But in face of all this, we finally landed safely with our gas gauge on empty and the crew completely exhausted.

To date we have one swastika and one periscope painted on our ship and hope that we can get some more. We are right in the thick of things over here and will probably have the opportunity.

The censorship on our letters is very strict here, but I will cite one incident that may get by. We were returning to our home base the other day alone, when some JU88's hit us out of the clouds and knocked out our two port engines. We got one of them on their second pass and then made for cloud cover before they could come around again. Fortunately, the clouds lasted for about an hour and we lost them completely. In order to maintain flying speed, we were forced to throw everything overboard that we did not need for ditching. To keep the ship straight, we had full right rudder trim tab and both the co-pilot and myself kept both feet on right rudder.

But by the grace of God and skill of our crew, we limped home and again landed safely on two engines. Later we discovered that some FW190's were dispatched to finish us off, but were intercepted by some (RAF) Beaufighters who engaged them long enough for us to get back.

Gotta save something for next time, so I'll quit now. Remember me to all my friends at the office and elsewhere and write often.

Sincerely,
'Oggie'

Bolin was overdue for promotion from 1st Lt. to Captain, having been in the grade for longer than normal. As there was no Captaincy available in the 66th squadron, a plan was devised to transfer him temporarily to the 506th sq. where there was a vacant position. There he would fly a few missions, be promoted to Captain and then transfer back to the 66th sq. His original crew including Merrill Berthrong and Art Grimes would stand down during his transfer.

2nd Lt. Orville Wulff of 506th sq. was due to be assigned his own crew, but instead he was ordered to fly as a co-pilot with Bolin.

Orville Wulff grew up in the town of De Smet in South Dakota where he, his sister and parents had moved from California in the 1920's. Ruth Swanson, Orville's sister, recounts his early years:

"My brother Orville was in De Smet during his teen years, assisting our dad in business. He went out to California where he worked until December 1941 when he volunteered into the US Air Force shortly after the Pearl Harbour incident. Orville graduated from Class 43-C of the Blackland Flying Army School of Waco, Texas at 9.00am on the morning of Saturday 20th March 1943, after which he made one more visit to our home in De Smet, before he was shipped overseas in August 1943.

84

Lt. Orville Wulff. His hat badge was only found
recently and has been returned to his sister.

Orville loved to fly and found a special world of
freedom way up there in the sky. He chose the Air Force:
"the safest branch of service to avoid capture" and "to live
in fame or go down in flame".

"When the war is over..." his plans were to become
a commercial pilot. One of his last letters said: "when
I get back to the USA, I will never leave that soil
again". His letters were always signed "Yours for
Victory!"

Ruth Swanson, November 1994.

Orville Wulff (on left) and colleague at The Blackland Flying
School.

Wulff's intended crew were passed to 1st Lt. Willard Michaels
who was a senior pilot acting as an assistant crew chief. He had not
flown many missions although an experienced pilot, and was
without a crew.

The new commanding officer of 506th sq. was Captain Robert E.
Kolliner. Soon after being appointed on the 14th January 1944, he
initiated a review of personnel requirements. There was much
unrest among the men of 506th sq. because of all the politics taking
place, including Bolin's transfer for promotion. Caught up in all of
this was Orville Wulff, who was re-classified from pilot to co-pilot.

Captain James McAtee of 506th sq. comments:

"After Kolliner ordered Michaels to fly combat, I scheduled him (Michaels) to go out three times. Each time Michaels aborted. The last time that it happened (2/2/44), he was met at his 'plane and told that he would be shipped out of the group,"

Orville Wulff with his fiancé taken in 1943.

Ollie C. Bowling was on 1st Lt. Michael's crew, he recollects:

"On that mission 2/2/44 with Lt Willard Michaels, we were at flight altitude when he lost control of the 'plane. When Michaels regained control we were down on the deck of the English Channel and returned to base. We as a crew, refused to fly with him again and he was transferred to the 91st Air Depot Group".

Orville was understandably very unhappy to make way for Michaels and Bolin, but they were more senior than he was.

Merrill Berthrong remembers meeting Orville:

> "Wulff sought me out over at our 66sq. Site. He wanted to know what sort of pilot Bolin was. He did not make a good impression with me, he seemed very nervous and apprehensive about combat flying. Of course all of the guys who flew were apprehensive to one degree or another, but to me he seemed excessively so. In light of what subsequently happened, perhaps his apprehension was not so extreme.
>
> I assured him that 'Oggie' was an excellent pilot, with vast experience and one who was cool and calm under stress".

On the 26th January 1944, Orville was presented with an Oak Leaf Cluster in addition to his Air Medal, previously awarded for 'exceptionally meritorious service while participating in bomber combat missions over enemy occupied Continental Europe' by Brig. Gen. Leon Johnson, commander of the 44th Bombardment Group. The citation also states that the Oak Leaf Cluster 'is in recognition of the courage, coolness and skill displayed by Lt. Wulff on these occasions'.

Wulff like Bolin had also been assigned to submarine patrol duties for six months when first arriving in England. Up until they joined the Bolin crew, both Orville Wulff and Harold Schwab the bombardier, had flown a number of missions with Captain James A. Bunce including raids to Compagne les Hesdin on Christmas Eve 1943, Ludwigshafen on the 30th December and St Jean D'Angely on New Years Eve.

The six enlisted men appointed to join the Bolin crew: – flight engineer T/Sgt James Bales from Dayton, Tennessee; radio operator Chester Yurick, Needham, Massachusetts; ball turret gunner S/Sgt James Wilson, Easley, Carolina; right waist gunner S/Sgt Aubrey Malloy, Hacoda, Alabama; left waist gunner, S/Sgt Ralph Strait,

Saluvia, Pennsylvania; tail gunner, S/Sgt George M. Dewald, Norristown, Pennsylvania; were transferred due to a quirk of fate. Their pilot, 1st Lt. Charles 'Chuck' Connor, had been indefinitely grounded in early January 1944 with an ear problem and his crew was broken up. 1st Lt. Connor did not resume flying duties until the following May and eventually survived the war.

Ralph Strait.

22-year-old Ralph Strait had made a remarkable recovery from his earlier life threatening injuries in November, when he was critically injured on a raid to Bremen. Esta Myers his widow, stated that Ralph was due to be sent home, but he insisted on staying on in England and rejoining his old crew mates so that they could finish their tour together.

1st Lt. Harold Schwab, that wry humoured individual from the Bronx, New York had survived the Ploesti raid when he was with 1st Lt. Whitlocks crew. Schwab now joined the Bolin crew to finish off his last few missions; likewise there was 2nd Lt. Edward Ackerman from Brooklyn, New York.

Don Chase remembers Harold Schwab:

"Harold or Schwab as he preferred to be called, was an original crewmate of mine and proved to be somewhat of a military maverick. Oh yes, he performed his bomb aiming duties with much care and competency, but his regimental bearing as a Commissioned Officer in the US Army Air Force was sometimes put aside in favour of individualism.

At times he neglected to pin on his Lieutenant bars. He didn't always button his shirt pockets. He'd just as soon fraternise with an enlisted man (like me) as he would with a fellow officer. He thought saluting, except perhaps for formal military occasions, was a waste of time and energy. Yes, Lt. Harold H.W.Schwab truly was a full time civilian in a part time military uniform. But as I say, he did his job very well indeed.

I first met Lt. Schwab at the Davis Montana Air Base at Tuscon, Arizona in December 1942, where he and eight other men led by pilot Lt. Charles Whitlock, were assigned as a crew to train on B-24's for combat duty. In May 1943 we left the USA for England. We took part in the air campaign over Sicily and Italy in June, after flying to Africa with 38 other crews of the 44th BG. Schwab was medically grounded with four others of our crew, when I and the remaining six crew, were shot down near Foggia, Italy. Schwab was returned to England.

When I eventually made it back to the UK, I was shortly thereafter transferred from the 506th to the 67th squadron. That move quashed any hopes that Schwab and I would fly together again.

I saw Schwab a couple of times on base before he went down on 'Ruth-Less'. At one chance meeting he invited me into the Officers Club for a drink. 'You know I can't do that; I'm a non-com, a sergeant' I said. 'Well you're A-2 jacket covers your stripes, so just stuff your cap in the pocket and walk in like you own the place'. And that's just what I did.

What a guy! With his wry humour and slow smile, he often brought a little sunshine into an otherwise damp, cloudy day.

When I learned of Harold Schwab's death, I felt saddened for quite a while. Even now I still think of him at times, I always will".

Don Chase, July 1995.

Chester Yurick.

It was on the 17th January 1944 that James Bolin officially joined the 506th squadron. The 21st January saw Bolin and his crew aboard 'Ruth-Less' as part of a nine-ship section to attack military installations at St Agatha, D'Aliermont, France. This time 506 sq. was following the 67th sq. but over France the section became separated from the lead group. Alone the 506th made four bombing runs on the target, which was extremely difficult to pick up because of fast moving cumulus clouds and the nature of the target. As the 44th Groups searched for a cloud break to locate their targets, a sharp engagement occurred between a few FW190's and the Liberators. Five B-24's were shot down including the lead ship.

Tragically, Major Anderson who had flown 'Ruth-Less' on her first mission nearly a year previously, was killed on this his last

Aubrey Maloy.

mission. As Commanding Officer of the 67th sq. and Command Pilot for this mission, he was mortally wounded by fragments from a flak burst which detonated in the bomb bay of his aircraft.

The following day 'Ruth-Less' had a generator replaced and on the 23rd January, Bolin and the crew flew off in her for some gunnery practice firing at white caps in the Wash. The 24th January mission returned early, having been recalled over England. The original target was military installations in Brussels, a total of eleven aircraft had taken off.

Further maintenance was carried out on 'Ruth-Less' that day including a reconfiguration of the ammunition to fire tracer every fourth instead of every fifth shot. The next day Lt's Wulff and Waino

On the 26th January 1944, Lt. Orville Wulff was awarded the Air Medal and Oak Leaf Cluster. Here Colonel Leon Johnson is presenting the Oak Leaf Cluster.

Hannuksela co-operatively flew two and a half-hours formation flying. Later that afternoon, 'Ruth-Less' had her Stewart-Warner heater return lines re-routed, to provide for more efficient heating at operations over 15,000 feet. All aircraft in the squadron had a complete changeover of ammunition, plus Y-282 had a modification completed to a main fuel cell vent on the port wing.

On the 26th January Lt. Wulff was reported to have flown a good formation during practice. Indeed there was much practice flying and the catching up with maintenance work at this time, as the weather over Germany was very poor. Thirteen of the twenty-nine missions flown during January and February were to CROSSBOW targets in France, where new crews and techniques were tried out with the added benefit of preventing or at least delaying the use of these installations by the Nazis.

Ten Liberators including 'Ruth-Less', were each loaded with 12 x 500 G.P. bombs for a raid to bomb a transportation centre in Frankfurt on the 29th. The Bolin crew was up early on the 30th when they faced another long and arduous mission over enemy territory, to strike at Brunswick. A record 778 bombers were dispatched. On the way, the group of 44th BG bombers became separated from the other force comprising of aircraft from the 392nd group which made up the 14th Combat Wing. Visibility had been forecast to be poor over Brunswick, when by chance a large break in the clouds revealed a choice target. The 44th BG took full advantage of this gift from nature and forty B-24's hammered a synthetic rubber production plant at Hanover as a target of opportunity.

Y-282 had left Shipdham at 09.02 hours for this raid and did not return until 15.04 hours, a distance of just over 1,100 miles was flown in total there and back. Between 12.40 and 13.15, forty to fifty JU88, FW190 and ME109 aircraft had attacked the formation. On the Interrogation Form completed by Bolin back at base, he states how a FW 190 attacked 'Ruth-Less' from one hundred yards in the 12 o'clock position and did a vertical dive out of the formation. It was also noted that the escorting P-47 Thunderbolt fighters had challenged the Luftwaffe 'planes head on, in an attempt to break up their attack.

It was observed how the Germans had also attacked the large American formation of bombers by the method of head on attack, as this had become the standard tactic for most front rank

Geschwadern. Attacking in Staffel strength of eight or nine at a time in line abreast, each wave would turn into the engagement from three to five miles ahead of the bombers. The best Luftwaffe pilots rolled their aircraft onto their backs as they pressed their attacks home, before diving violently away at the last moment under the bombers.

'Ruth-Less' despite her relative age and combat weariness, had demonstrated good serviceability throughout January. After that last tough mission to Hanover, 'Oggie' and his crew must have felt more relaxed at the prospect of a 'Milk Run' mission, to hit a NOBALL site in the Pas de Calais. These trips were euphemistically christened 'Milk Runs' by the aircrews, because there was usually little time spent over enemy territory to and from the target. However these missions had become anything but 'Milk Runs' since they were first targeted in August 1943. The Germans quickly moved in additional rail mounted heavy anti-aircraft flak batteries around the V1 installations, which caused the bombing altitude to be raised to 20,000 feet. The 'ski ramp' launching sites were so small, as to be virtually impossible to hit from this height and it was not unusual for intrepid bomb group commanders to take their formations over the targets on three, four or even more runs.

The boast that the USAAF could hit a pickle barrel from high altitude within a fifty foot practice circle on a dry lake at Muroc, California, was proving harder to emulate in the less than perfect conditions prevailing in the European Theatre of Operations.

Chapter 8

WATTEN – THE MILK RUN
THAT TURNED SOUR

ITLER made it an absolute top priority, that work to develop the secret V1, V2 and V3 terror weapons should proceed with all haste. The Vergeltungswaffe 1 (Revenge Weapon 1) or Fieseler 103 Kirschkern (Cherry Stone), was a small pilotless aircraft powered by a pulse jet engine. It had an automatic gyroscopic navigational instrument system similar to but a much cruder version of, the Inertia Navigation System as found on modern commercial jet aircraft. The direction of the flying bomb was governed automatically by the gyroscope, which gave signals to the air-operated rudder and elevator. Directional information was obtained from a pre-set compass, the air-log measured the flight distance as set before firing. When the programmed distance was achieved, the elevators were depressed and the bomb dived towards the ground. The warhead contained 1,870lbs of high explosive, which detonated on impact.

The pulse engines had a very distinctive 'throbbing' sound to them, anyone who noticed one flying overhead would be struck by terror if the motor was heard to cut out. Around ten to twelve seconds later there would be a terrific explosion, but where? You wouldn't know until perhaps it was too late. The introduction of much faster Allied fighter aircraft like the Hawker Tempest, which could intercept these flying bombs and shoot them down, saved many lives. One Tempest pilot developed the tactic of flying alongside a V1, putting the wing of his aircraft under that of the flying bomb, and by pushing up the wing of the V1 would cause the gyro-navigation system of the 'Doodlebug' to topple, thus ensuring it went out of control and crashed. Lines of large barrage balloons circled London and batteries of anti-aircraft guns ringed the southern suburbs of London to diminish the V1 threat.

The V2, or A4 terror weapon as it was previously known, was a true rocket born explosive system which was being developed at Peenemunde. The V3 was a three barrelled, 50mm artillery piece capable of firing six hundred tons of high explosive into the heart of London ninety miles away from Mimoyecques in the Pas de Calais. Fortunately the Allied invasion overtook the work on this particular weapon, although more recently President Saddam Hussein of Iraq initiated a project to build a multi-charge pump action supergun, using identical technology to which the Nazis pioneered in WW2.

After the war, it was discovered that there was a plan to use a piloted version of the V1 as a suicide bomb, which was named the V4. Two hundred of these V4's were produced but they were never used, as Hitler paradoxically found the thought of Germans flying suicide missions morally reprehensible.

Hitler believed that when his V1 bombs started to reign down on Britain as part of his 'Steinbok' or 'Baby Blitz' offensive, the population would soon become demoralised. Fortunately developmental problems delayed the anticipated 'Rocket Blitz' until the 6th June 1944, but the launch sites and storage bunkers were already targets of the utmost importance by the beginning of the year.

Bolin's first three missions with the 66th sq. had been on the Liberator B-24H model. Although a later design, the heavier nose turret caused the centre of gravity to shift forward and make the 'H' version even trickier to fly. Also the increased weight reduced its performance somewhat, so 'Ruth-Less' being an early 'D' model must have seemed like a hot ship in comparison.

At Shipdham, Bolin and his crew were roused from their beds in the freezing cold Nissen huts for breakfast, after which followed a briefing for Mission 166. There was the usual buzz of whispered comments from the crews as the Briefing Officer drew back the curtain on the display board revealing the target for that day and the routes depicted by coloured ribbon to and from it.

The huge V1 assembly building at Foret d'Eperlecques, Watten in the Pas de Calais, was the world's largest bunker and 130,000 tons of reinforced concrete went into its construction. The construction of the bunker was very similar to the Nazi U-boat pens on the west coast of France. The roof and sidewalls were extremely thick and impervious to the 2,000 lb bombs. This was well known to the planners of the mission, and the ultimate aim therefore was to make the surrounding area of the bunker so cratered, that only a mountain goat could get in and out. It was not until the British scientist Barnes Wallis developed his 'earthquake' bombs which penetrated under the bunkers before detonating, that they were finally destroyed.

Some thirty crews would fly the mission for the 44th BG, backed up by four spares who would take the place of any early aborts to the target. On the Briefing Check Form for the mission which was distributed to all the pilots showing their position in the formation, 'Ruth-Less' has been placed on the outside edge of the front right hand side echelon with Lt. Borkoski in Liberator Z153 in front and 1st Lt. Willard Michaels immediately on the left in Q965.

Colonel Dexter Hodge, the Commanding Officer of the 66th sq., would be the Pathfinder leader for the group on this mission. Hodge had participated in the Ploesti raid and was one of a handful of survivors flying that day. A quietly spoken yet authoritative Texan, he always made a point of flying with crews when they were on the last mission of their 'tour', as he was considered to be lucky. At around 11.05 hours, the Liberators each carrying four 2,000 lb bombs, began taking off from Shipdham. Assembling of the groups of aircraft was affected with difficulty due to multi-layered cloud, high winds and severe icing conditions. Altogether four B-24 groups totalling 113 aircraft despite the handicaps of the weather, departed the assembly point over Beachy Head on the Sussex coast on schedule and headed south-east across the Channel.

There was one G.H (ground radar) equipped aircraft in each group. Four of the bombers including Q965 commanded by 1st Lt. Michaels had to abort. The four groups of aircraft were divided into two forces and followed the ordered routes to their respective targets. The rendezvous with the P47 Thunderbolt fighters, who provided close support and protection to the bombers was initiated according to plan.

Whilst the other force of bombers went to St Pol / Siracourt, Bolin and his two groups proceeded to Watten. The weather was dreadful over France too and the Watten groups used the G.H. pathfinder equipment to bomb through the overcast. The aircraft were at an altitude of 18,000 feet and the outside air temperature was minus twenty degrees centigrade. Over the target area moderate and accurate flak was encountered and many ships in the formation suffered minor damage. Bolin with his group was compelled to make another bombing run, due to interference caused when the first group of bombers turned inside at the I.P. (Initial Point) and approached the target on a course which was in conflict with the others. To avoid this confrontation and the possibility of collision, Bolin's group made a second run on the target. By now they were some twenty-two minutes behind schedule.

Based on reports given to surviving family members and statements from crew in accompanying aircraft, the following account is as accurate as one can describe of the events concerning 'Ruth-Less'.

The German flak batteries using their ground radar guided 88mm and 110mm guns, bracketed 'Ruth-Less' and it was during the second run that she was hit. The flak shell exploded by the starboard wing, knocking out number three engine. Bolin and Wulff quickly feathered the propeller to prevent it windmilling and causing excessive drag. Losing number three engine was critical, as this motor powered the hydraulic pump responsible for the hydraulic pressure which operated the flaps and landing gear. 'Ruth-Less' continued on her attack run and dropped her bombs on the Watten installation. Altogether the fifty Liberators attacking Watten dropped a total of 191 tons of high explosives.

It soon became apparent to Bolin and the crew, that the flak burst had also damaged the number four engine, causing it to stream oil. As precious power was nursed out of that engine, 'Ruth-Less' was observed to drop back and become separated from the formation. With his previous experience of flying a B-24 on two engines, Bolin realised that they would not make it back to Shipdham. To further add to their problems, the aircraft's primary flight instruments had failed. With the artificial horizon unserviceable and flying in cloud, Bolin and Wulff would not be able to ascertain the attitude of the aircraft without a visual reference. They had no option but to descend out of the overcast and head for the nearest landfall in the UK.

Lt. Art Grimes was navigating aboard Lt. Milliners Liberator which also encountered difficulties, he recalls:

"Several of our aircraft were hit as we left the French coast. Our crew lost all directional control of the 'plane, but fortunately we were headed for England. Milliner opted to stay with the aircraft and felt we could reach England, at which time we would abandon the 'plane".

Walt Milliner adds:

"Flak had taken out my rudder controls and the number one engine. The prop would not feather. RAF Sea Rescue stood by as we made it across the Channel to Ramsgate".

Grimes recollects:

"We reached the English Coast and Milliner and I ordered all the enlisted crew members, plus the bombardier officer who was on his last mission, to bail out. After ensuring that all the crew had left the aircraft except for Milliner and his co-pilot Merrill Berthrong, I went to the rear of the aircraft and bailed out as well. I was not injured but almost hit a cow as I landed in a pasture near a RAF fighter field. I was observed landing by a gentleman driving a small car and he picked me up as I was rolling my 'chute up. He drove me to the fighter base where the RAF treated me royally.

I found out after I had bailed out, that Milliner decided that he had a small amount of directional control left using the trim tab controls of the auto-pilot. He and Berthrong opted to land the aircraft at Manston in Kent. They succeeded, but unfortunately the 'plane destroyed a communications van at the end of the runway, killing Sgt Cross, the RAF controller. Milliner once stated to me that they had descended so quickly that the thick plexiglas windows of the cockpit had become so badly iced up, that he made virtually a blind landing".

Whilst Merrill Berthrong was still contemplating his close call with death or injury, his old friend and flying partner was struggling at the controls of 'Ruth-Less'. Bolin had set a course back across the Channel, but for some reason either intentionally or not, had taken a more westerly heading than Milliner and Berthrong.

When they eventually made landfall, it was west of the seaside town of Eastbourne close to Beachy Head, which had been the original rendezvous point that morning. It is still a matter of conjecture why Bolin and Wulff had taken this longer westerly route over the Channel, perhaps it was just a coincidence. However both pilots appear to have been aware of the grass A.L.G. (Advanced Landing Ground) satellite fighter airfield at Gayles Farm, situated near the village of Friston between Eastbourne and Seaford and were obviously heading for it. Did they note its existence earlier that day as they were circling over Beachy Head, or was it already known to them as an emergency airfield?

Friston Field today.

As the huge B-24 lined up for its approach to land, startled ground personnel at Friston fired red Very flares to warn Bolin off from landing at this time, due to congestion on the field. 'Oggie' initiated

Nose art from 'Heaven Can Wait', a B-24H Liberator of the 68th Sq., Shipdham.

a gentle arcing turn taking 'Ruth-Less' parallel with the cliffs at Beachy Head and then round over Eastbourne's seafront near the pier.

Whilst coaxing power out of number four engine, Bolin and Wulff consulted their maps. From the north westerly direction they were now heading across Eastbourne, Bolin could see that they must make a left turn to approach the Friston field. This meant negotiating the long stretch of hills known as the South Downs, which run from the west of Eastbourne in a northerly direction. Bolin's options were limited, he could have ditched 'Ruth-Less' close to the seashore. However B-24's had a tendency to break-up on impact with water, due to water rushing in through the roller-shutter bomb bay doors and breaking the main spar, which would cause the aircraft to rapidly sink. Maybe one or more of the men had been badly injured by the flak burst so Bolin had decided to carry on?

Another option was to belly land the aircraft on the fields around the outskirts of Eastbourne. Bolin and Wulff must have been confident that number four engine would hold out and they would make Friston, where emergency services and medical facilities would be immediately to hand.

B-24H 'Heaven Can Wait' crashed and burned on the 12th March 1944 at Friston, on the return from bombing a target at Siracourt, France.

The airfield at Gayles Farm comprised of a 'V' shaped grass landing area that ran 5,000 feet in a south westerly direction directly to a cliff top and the sea below. Friston had Hurricanes of No's: 253 and 32 squadrons stationed there initially from June 1942, a month after it was officially reopened as a frontline fighter base. From the 10th November 1943, Spitfire VB's of the Belgian 349 squadron were flying out of Friston along with the Polish 308 (Krakowski) Squadron who flew Spitfire 1X's.

Because of its conspicuous situation on top of the cliffs known as the Seven Sisters, Friston was frequently the choice of bomber crews desperate to land their crippled bombers. Landing a stricken aircraft the size of 'Ruth-Less' on that muddy field, was going to demand all of Bolin's skill and experience. Many other large bombers had made emergency landings there before and there was no reason why 'Oggie' couldn't pull it off.

Twenty seven year old Chester Yurick the radio operator, was on his last mission. Soon he hoped it would be all over so that he could return home and marry his fiancé in Needham. The crew willed number four engine to keep going, as it popped and backfired intermittently. The strong winds buffeted the aircraft as it flew at only roof top height across the Ocklynge and Old Town areas of Eastbourne. The waist gunners peered out of their positions and waved at the people below. Arthur King was in his back garden in Victoria Drive when 'Ruth-Less' flew over:

> "It was making a terrible racket, I could hear the engines roaring and I wondered if they would make it. They had a lot of height to make up."

As she pushed her baby son Malcolm along Victoria Drive, Mrs Delphie Parsons listened intently to the throbbing sound of aero engines as the Liberator approached. The engine note sounded uneven as moments later, the bomber like a huge ghostly spectre, staggered over the rooftops. The cloud base was low and in the mist Delphie thought how eerie it looked as the bomber loomed from the haze, appearing to fly so slowly. As 'Ruth-Less' passed over, she clearly saw several airmen waving and shouting to her out of the waist windows, she waved back and uttered a silent prayer.

Derek Wilkinson then a schoolboy, was enjoying a break period outside of the clubhouse on Willingdon Golf course, which had been utilised as a temporary school for children who had not been evacuated from the town. German hit and run attacks had forced the pupils of his school to be moved further inland to a safer area. The clubhouse nestled at the foot of the Downs, which at this vicinity rise nearly six hundred feet. When Derek saw the Liberator approaching, he realised with horror that unless it gained height it would be too low to escape the mist-capped hill ahead. Other eyewitnesses reported that two of the engines were not operational and a propeller was twisted.

Alan Caffyn was a lad of ten at the time he was walking up Willingdon Road with his mother when the aircraft came overhead:

> "I will always remember the chap who appeared standing in the doorway of the aircraft, and I could see him thinking, do I jump or don't I."

With the Downs running along his left side and a spur of a hill known as Butts Brow jutting out in front of him, Bolin was boxed in. Pilots have a macabre term for this type of situation - 'Coffin Corner'. Unable to turn sharply without stalling, his only choice was to outclimb the cloud-veiled hill in front of him. 'Oggie' firewalled the two good engines and powered up number four engine for all it was worth. Would it be enough? How high did the hill go? Bolin and Wulff must have been very concerned, as they lost sight of the ground below?

Up on the Downs was Land Army girl Audrey Armstrong along with Ned, the green keeper for the Willingdon Golf Club. They were rounding up sheep when they heard the ever present and distinctive throbbing sound of aircraft engines approaching them. The swirling mist was so dense, that they could only see a few yards ahead of them and the sheep bleated ever more loudly, as if they sensed the impending danger. The animals scattered as the thunder reached a crescendo. Suddenly 'Ruth-Less' reared-up in a final desperate attempt to avoid her fate as she roared into view, the vapours clung to her drab green painted fuselage as if she was coated in a film of ectoplasm. Quickly the grassy hill rushed up under her as she creaked and shuddered in an unaccustomed fashion to the men within, as if to indicate that she was exhausted and nothing more could now be done to prevent the inevitable. It was then that Y-282 hit the hilltop, the time of the impact was 15.45 hours.

The Liberator's plexiglass nose crumpled against the solid chalk, barely covered by a thin layer of grass and soil. When the aircraft struck the hillside, the crew were thrown from their positions as the fuselage ruptured. In that briefest of moments, no longer than it takes for a flash of lightning, their deepest and most basic instinct made the airmen aware that death was upon them.

The crash scene showing the complete destruction of 'Ruth-Less' so near to the hill top.

'Ruth-Less' stood on her nose for a moment, as she was pole-vaulted over onto her back in an awry and violent cartwheel, only thirty feet below the brow of the hill and probable safety. As she came crashing down the airframe totally disintegrated, throwing off the engines as the wings separated from the fuselage. The fuel tank cells ruptured and the 100 octane petrol was instantaneously ignited by the heat of the engines. A huge fireball erupted as the hilltop was scorched and blackened from the fiery inferno. Wreckage and bodies lay scattered over a large area.You could not recognise the mass of twisted and broken debris as ever being an aeroplane. So complete was the destruction, that only the twin fins were left partially intact as indicators that a Liberator had crashed there.

John Punyer, who was playing truant from school with a friend, was also up on the hill when he heard 'Ruth-Less' crash. They had been up there scouring the Butts Brow area for pieces of plexiglass from dog-fighting aircraft. He recalls:

"My friend and I were on the hill close to where the aircraft crashed. When we heard the explosion we both ran round to the site of the impact. The hillside is very steep and scrambling down one side away from the fire was one of the American crewmen. He was hobbling badly and we could see that one of his legs had been severed above the knee. We called to him as he slid down the embankment to the apparent safety of the Bridle Path below. As he rested there for a moment, one of the aircraft's engines broke free from what was left of a wing and before he could get away, it rolled on top of him.

We ran straight home and for many years I had night-mares about what I had witnessed happen to that poor airman".

John Punyer, October 1994.

Two days later when heavy lifting equipment was removing the larger pieces of wreckage, Orville Wulff's body was recovered from under that engine.

Private Thomas Jones was with a detachment of REME engineers working on vehicles at the Ratton Manor Estate below, when the cry went out that an aircraft had crashed:

"I and another soldier got into a Jeep and raced up the Bridle Path until we reached the wreckage. Most of the American airmen had appalling injuries, but we found one (Chester Yurick) who was still alive. We carried him to the Jeep and drove to the Princess Alice Memorial Hospital. Apart from a round hole in his forehead, he appeared relatively unscathed. We hung around a couple of hours until when the Sister came out and told us that he had died. Apparently he never regained consciousness".

Thomas Jones, May 1995.

Fire Officer Albert Jones was stationed behind the Queens Hotel on Eastbourne's seafront when he was alerted of the crash. He and his fellow firemen tried to get their tender close to the wreckage:

"There wasn't much that we could do, save putting out the isolated pockets of fire which burned for some time in the gloom of the swirling mist. We got our machine as near as we could to the crash site, but it was still some distance below in the Bridle Path.

After putting out the fires, it was our duty to remove the bodies of the crew. I remember looking at those American airmen and being impressed with their standard of uniform and equipment. They were all wearing flak jackets and some had silk neck scarves. Because the hill-side was so steep, the only way to get the bodies down was by carefully rolling them. As we did this, one of the airmen started to gasp. He was immediately given heart massage by an army officer, but his efforts to revive this poor young man failed".

Albert Green, May 1995.

The ten airmen were initially buried in the American Cemetery at Brookwood, near Woking in Surrey. After the war, the bodies of seven of the crew were repatriated to the USA. Orville Wulff's letter stating that when he got back to the USA he would never leave that

Orville Wulff was re-buried with full military honours.

soil again, prompted his family to have his remains brought back. He was re-buried during 1948 with full military honours at a ceremony conducted in the Fort Snelling National Cemetery, Minnesota. Six other bodies of the crew were exhumed and removed to the USA for family burials.

'Oggie' Bolin, Ralph Strait and Chester Yurick were re-interred at the same time in the American Military Cemetery at Maddingly near Cambridge.

'Ruth-Less' was considered a veteran aircraft. She and her crews had participated in some of the longest and toughest missions flown by the 8th USAAF. Yet wounded and compromised by the loss of two engines and with no instruments to guide her crew, she finally succumbed to the vicious embrace of that hillside overlooking Eastbourne. It was her 39th mission.

Bolin's crew became another sad statistic in the 'Flying Eightball's'

1st Lt. Orville Wulff's grave.

necrology. During 1943 and the first half of 1944, B-24 accidents resulted in 432 complete wrecks, with an estimated cost then of U$142 million and 1,672 fatalities. The 44th Bombardment Group's share of this was 324 casualties in 1944, rising to 1,725, including 859 men killed in action when the war ended in 1945.

The bunker at Watten was never completely put out of action by bombing alone. Only the Allied invasion of France finally terminated the V1 menace.

Merrill Berthrong attended the funeral of his friend James Bolin in February 1944 and visited the grave again in 1990. Bolin's original crew in the 66th sq. including Berthrong and Grimes, was broken up on his death. Berthrong became the 66th sq. Operations Officer and Art Grimes who, during that hectic first week in February 1944, survived three crash landings and a bail out. He too has visited 'Oggies' grave twice in recent years.

Chapter 9
FIFTY YEARS LATER

RESEARCHING the history of 'Ruth-Less', her crews and the 506th sq. in general has been extremely time consuming and I must admit that writing a book is one of the most challenging tasks which I have ever undertaken. It is now February 2000 and still I am adding new material and correcting the old.

In the summer of 1994, I pondered how Arthur King has kept the memory of the 'Ruth-Less' crew alive for all these years. As each year passed he was finding it more difficult to make his annual pilgrimage up there onto the Downs. Perhaps a permanent memorial could be placed at the crash site, but how would you raise the money and go about obtaining the necessary planning permission? Would people merely say after 50 years 'it hasn't been done before in all this time, why bother now?'

Ruth Swanson informed me that her family was given very little information by the US authorities, regarding the circumstances of her brother Orville's death. It was highly probable that the other relatives of the crew were also unaware due to official secrecy at the time, what had led to the deaths of their loved ones, other than the men had died somewhere in the European Theatre of Operations. Should I try and contact the other relatives, or would I merely be raking over and unearthing the bad memories of the past? Ruth gave me encouragement to pursue the matter, so during August 1994 I set about writing to the head-postmasters of all the home towns listed on a M.A.C.R (Missing Air Crew Report) where each of the crew had resided prior to joining the airforce. This is how Ruth had been traced, but she had lived in a relatively small town and it was a stroke of luck that the postmaster remembered that the family had moved away from De Smet to Lake Preston, South Dakota after the war.

This line of investigation did not provide any leads, I never heard another thing from any of the postmasters. George Dixon and I met one evening, and I discussed my idea about establishing a permanent memorial to the crew. We investigated the likely problems that we might encounter, but with the V.E. Day celebrations and commemorations planned for 1995 in the UK, we deduced that it would be a most appropriate time to have a memorial dedicated to the crew of 'Ruth-Less'.

Councillor Ron Parsons was Eastbourne's Mayor during 1994/95 and little did I know at the time, it was his mother who had waved to the crew of 'Ruth-Less' as she pushed her pram along Victoria Drive on the afternoon the aircraft crashed. I wrote to him on the 22nd of October 1994 about the proposals George and I suggested for a memorial. A week later Cllr. Parsons replied most enthusiastically about the project and offered his wholehearted support.

In mid November, a meeting was arranged with the Downland Advisory Committee up on the Downs at the crash site, to discuss the memorial and to see what was feasible. The original concept of a flint built seating arrangement with a brass plaque was thrown out. Eventually a granite memorial about the size of a cartwheel laid horizontally appeared to be the most favoured option. Well I thought, how big is a cartwheel, perhaps there is an opportunity here for a bit of artistic licence?

So when I drew the first rough sketch for the memorials design, it was to a scale that would eventually dictate a size of around 4'6" by 3'6". George wondered if a memorial that big would get by the Downland Advisory Committee. I mentioned to George that it could always be made smaller, enlarging it would be a more difficult proposition. My sketch was submitted to Jefferson Collard, the Historic Buildings Advisor for Eastbourne Borough Council. Jefferson did a fantastic job professionally interpreting my drawing by computer and working out a specification for its design and construction.

It was George who came up with the inscription 'Our Friends and Allies Far From Home' and Jeff suggested that the lettering should be polished and raised, with the background a slightly rough and matt finish. Once the final proof had been approved, another full size version was made for the computerised etching of the Norwegian granite face.

A stonemason in Brighton had provided a ballpark figure of how much our memorial was likely to cost and quoted £1,800. Allowing for unforeseen incidentals a target of £2,000 was set, a 'Ruth-Less' Memorial Fund bank account was established with George as the treasurer and I as the secretary. We were also the committee for the project, as we had been advised to 'keep it small'. So far so good, but how would we go about raising the money? Some publicity for the project was required, so I contacted our local newspaper, the Eastbourne Herald who had run the original story about Arthur King. Reporter Maria Brooks thought the memorial was a great idea too and was intrigued by the story of the Liberator. A week later she duly obliged by writing a substantial article in the sister paper of the Herald, the Eastbourne Gazette.

Many letters in support of the project appeared in later editions of both newspapers buoyed us. Mayor Parsons was instrumental in assisting me to locate surviving family members of the crew, by writing to all the mayors in the US of the hometowns which I had listed. In the 'States it is only the larger cities which have mayors, but some of the letters were passed to local historical societies and newspapers. Soon my telephone was ringing as newspaper reporters from the US picked up the story and offered to do everything they could to help. Mayor Parsons then sent out a further volley of letters addressed to the State Governors of the areas from which the crew originated. This time we hit the jackpot as we were quickly advised that the families of several of the crew had been found and contacted.

It was great news and since the first article in the local paper, subsequent features and replies to letters sent to local organisations, had initiated a considerable flow of money into the 'Ruth-Less' fund. As the relatives of the crew were found, I fired off letters containing an abridged history of the events which led to the crash of 'Ruth-Less'. Initially a few of the relatives were incredulous and surprised to say the least, that after so long such a project was being undertaken.

Needham, Massachusetts is a suburb of Boston and the hometown of Chester Yurick, the radio operator on 'Ruth-Less'. His sister Stella, still lived at the same address as that given for her brother. Now in her early eighties, Stella proved to be a typically feisty American senior citizen with a real zest for life when I initially telephoned her. Linda Rosencrance, a reporter on *The Needham Times* had picked up on the 'Ruth-Less' story and had an article printed about it. Linda set up a fund to raise money for the memorial and tentatively it was planned that Stella would be able to travel to the UK for the dedication ceremony.

A Commissioner in Mercesburg, Fulton County, Pennsylvania named Robert Garloch found Esta Myers, the widow of Ralph Strait in February 1995. All of this was a complete surprise to her. After the war she had re-married but still lived in the area. Upon Ralph's death, she told me that the Veteran's Administration of the USAAF had informed her that his aircraft had been shot down over Watten. Because of that, she and his family did not request to have his remains repatriated, as they did not think there was much of him to bring back! The first she knew about the circumstances of the crash was in that February, some 51 years later. She wrote to me in March '95:

> "It was quite a shock learning this after so many years, but the sentiment is still there".

During February, planning permission was granted for the memorial. Mayor Ron Parsons, Arthur King and I gave an interview for Meridian Television at that time, which gave the memorial project further impetus and prompted a surge of contributions. Sitting in front of the television at his daughter's home in Ashford, Kent one evening was Thomas Jones, who took Chester Yurick to hospital. When the feature about 'Ruth-Less' was aired, he wrote to Mayor Parsons about his involvement in the tragedy.

Will Lundy, the historian of the 44th BG, informed me that he and a party of veterans would be visiting the UK during May to take part in the VE Day commemorations. As they would be staying on for over a week more, they planned to make the trip to Eastbourne on Saturday the 13th May, which was the date now set for the dedication of the memorial. Arrangements and plans for the service were now being organised at a furious pace. There was so much to take account of, from car parking to what religious faiths would be represented and a hundred other things. In the meantime the memorial specification was sent out for tender and eventually a local firm was awarded the contract.

The main concern for George and I was whether we would raise sufficient funds to cover the cost of the monument. We were too committed now to let the project fail merely through a lack of funds and were resigned to making up the shortfall ourselves if necessary. Our fears were soon allayed when some substantial donations from America put us within striking distance of our target. Everything was going well, better than we could have dreamed of, all we needed now was fine weather on the day of the dedication.

The memorial had been constructed and the contractors were ready to put it in position. George, Jefferson Collard and I went back up onto the Downs to mark out the exact spot where the monument would be placed. It was a perfect day when the contractors turned up with the memorial and carefully lifted it from the back of the lorry to its final resting spot. The large granite tablet with its substantial concrete plinth weighed several tons, and a degree of excavation had to be carried out to bed in the foundations. A wooden protective shroud was built over and around the memorial until the day of its unveiling. Surplus funds from the memorial account paid for a ten year comprehensive insurance policy, after which Eastbourne Borough Council will assume responsibility for the memorial.

I had almost given up all hope of any of the relatives travelling to England for the ceremony. Ruth Swanson was too infirm for such a long journey and likewise Esta Myers. Near the end of March, Linda Rosencrance of The Needham Times telephoned me to say that Stella Myshrall was coming. British Airways through their Charities Division assisted with the cost of the airfare, the rest was made up from donations sent to The Needham Times. Stella had never left the shores of mainland USA before, so to undertake such an adventure at her stage of life, was indeed an example of her spirit and determination to represent her brother.

Stella Myshrall arrived at Heathrow Airport on her flight from Boston on Wednesday the 10th May and George travelled up to meet her, as I unfortunately couldn't avoid a flying duty to Dallas that same day. It was late evening back home in the UK when I eventually 'phoned home from Texas, to check that everything was well with Stella. My mother told me that she was 'absolutely lovely' and that she had already gone to bed. Greatly relieved, I got changed out of my uniform and settled down to write my speech for the coming Saturday.

It seemed appropriate that Stella should stay with my parents in their house backing onto the Downs. A few days before the dedication ceremony, Stella went up to the crash site with a container of soil, half of which she spread over the area where her brother had died. She had collected this soil from a spot on the riverbank back at Needham, where her brother Chester loved to fish. The rest of the contents she spread over his grave at Maddingly, when taken there a few days later by George Dixon and in the company of Col. John D. Marr, an official representative from her brother's home town of Needham.

Stella Myshrall sprinkling soil, taken from the river bank
back in Needham where her brother loved to fish,over the crash site

George Dixon standing on what is left of the dispersal point
at Shipdham assigned to 'Ruth-Less'.

The weather in England during the first two weeks of May was unseasonably warm. Some of the American veterans were Californians and felt quite at home in the balmy temperatures and azure blue skies. Of course it was just our luck that the weather was forecast to break by the weekend, but my faith in Eastbourne's reputation as the 'Suntrap of the South' was not unfounded.

George and I travelled up to Shipdham on the previous Monday to look around the old aerodrome and to meet the veterans from the 44th B.G, who were going to the Arrow Air clubhouse later in the afternoon for a barbecue. It was a wonderful experience to see these American crewmen still sporting their original leather flying jackets, with the graffiti type drawings on their backs of the aircraft they flew. To me they were like living history. It was a unique opportunity to talk with veterans whose names I had researched and studied on Interrogation Forms or Briefing CheckLists. They in turn were looking forward to their Eastbourne trip, to be part of the ceremony and witness another piece of their wartime heritage being preserved for posterity.

Arthur King stepping forward to unveil the 'Ruth-Less' memorial.

So finally the day arrived when all of the hard work by so many different people was culminated. The weather was kind to us although the odd cloud looked a little threatening. By 1.45 pm a large crowd of at least 400 people had already gathered. The boys and girls of the local Air Training Corps were directing the traffic into the car parks and assisting people along the way, to the cordoned area around the memorial. Ten minutes before the ceremony was due to start, the band of the Royal British Legion started to play and there was a frisson of anticipation amongst everyone gathered

118

Stella Myshrall with Arthur King.

(From left to right) Harry Roberts, B-24 Flight Engineer; Richard 'Dick' Butler,
B-24 pilot; the author, 'Will' Lundy, B-24 Crew Chief and historian for the
44th Bombardment Group Veterans Association.

Arthur King with Eastbourne Mayor Ron Parsons.

there, as his worship Mayor Parsons accompanied by his wife, Stella Myshrall and the Deputy Mayor, Maurice Skilton, took their places.

The monument had been covered with an American flag and centred on top was the bloodstained folded hat of 1st Lt. Orville Wulff, which was found in his breast pocket when he died. Veterans of the Royal British Legion made a fine sight as they lined the perimeter, their standards proudly raised with the town of Eastbourne as a backdrop. It was an Ecumenical service with three ministers participating led by the Reverend Doug McAvoy. Also attending was Eastbourne's Member of Parliament, Nigel Waterson. The American ambassador was represented by Lt. Col. Snukis of the US Marines, who made a speech reminding us of past sacrifices made so that we can be free today.

After the first hymn O' Valiant Heart, I addressed the crowd to briefly outline the circumstances that led to the crash of 'Ruth-Less,' after which I invited Arthur King to step forward and have the honour of unveiling the memorial. As Arthur rolled back the Stars and Stripes flag, a few large raindrops started to fall and Stella Myshrall later remarked of these 'teardrops from heaven'. Right on cue just as the ceremony ended, aircraft of the RAF's Red Arrows display team roared overhead dipping their wings in salute.

Following the ceremony on the Downs, most people moved to a reception hosted by the Mayor in Eastbourne Town Hall, where a backdrop of photographs and pictures had been assembled to illustrate the 'Ruth-Less' story. Visitors, especially those from the United States, were welcomed by the Mayor and George Dixon.

As I close this book nearly five years after the ceremony, I have yet again enjoyed a bracing walk on a bright winter's day to visit the memorial. I am touched by more fresh flowers laid at the foot of the stone and the few sentimental words written by an anonymous well wisher, left fluttering in the breeze as a symbol of remembrance for sacrifices made, by our friends and Allies far from home.

Yes, we will remember the Bolin crew . . .

POSTSCRIPT

FRANK SLOUGH survived the war, but was killed soon after it in a training exercise whilst flying in the USA.

Ray Lacombe was upgraded to the left seat on his return from Africa with 'Ruth-Less'. On his 25th mission, he and his crew bailed out over Switzerland where they were interned. However he managed to 'jump the fence,' joined the Maquis and after the invasion returned home. After retiring from the US Air Force as a Colonel in 1966, he immediately joined the Boeing Company in New Orleans. At Boeing he worked on the development of the first stage of the Saturn rocket project. Later he joined Martin-Marietta Aerospace Company and was instrumental in the design of the external fuel

Colonel Ray Lacombe.

tank for the Space Shuttle. He finally retired for good in 1985 and resides in Slidell, Louisiana.

James Caillier also worked for Boeing after the war and was involved in the Titan missile project. He too is happily retired living in Sumner, Washington State and Queen Creek, near Phoenix, Arizona where he spends the winter months. He and his wife Jean still dance regularly every Wednesday and Saturday.

In May 1997 veterans of the 44th Bombardment Group came to Eastbourne for two days as part of their European Tour including James Caillier. A service was held around the memorial and later that evening a banquet in honour of the American veterans took place at the Lansdowne Hotel, hosted by Councillor Ron Parsons. Also there was Councillor Parsons mother Delphie, who had around her neck a crucifix fashioned from the plexiglass found at the crash site of 'Ruth-Less', and which she has worn ever since.

Lt. Harold Schwab's father remarried after the war and from that union, another son was produced who was also named Harold. Harold junior was never told by his father that he had an elder half brother.

Harold Schwab is a high-powered lawyer and senior partner of a large law firm on the Broadway, New York. He only found out about his older sibling in 1997. Harold was in Niagara representing a large car company in a liability lawsuit, when during a break from the proceedings, a work colleague wandered into a local bookstore. In there he found a book written by Martin Bowman entitled 'Thunder in the Heavens'. He just happened to thumb through and noticed the name Harold Schwab in a paragraph about a mission that 'Ruth-Less' participated in. He bought the book and showed it to Harold.

Not long after, Harold wrote to Martin Bowman and a copy was sent on to the author, who then contacted Harold and from a letter dated November 1997 he states:

"I am sure it is not merely coincidental that both my father had possessed a dry sense of humour (as do I) which was apparently the hallmark of my brother. Further, when I was USAF First Lieutenant in JAG (1957 - 1959) I was certainly viewed as a rebel but never-theless received the highest ratings possible. I gather Harold W. was the same.

BIBLIOGRAPHY

Flying Start, *Sir Hugh Dundas*

Jane's Fighting Aircraft of World War II

The Mighty Eighth, *Roger Freeman.*

Eighth Airforce Bomber Stories, *Ian MacLachlan.*

The Mare's Nest, *David Irving.*

Inside the Third Reich, *Albert Speer.*

INDEX